Raised Right in the South

Rose Elaine Lumley Brantley

To order additional copies of this book, contact:
Xlibris Corporation
1-888-795-4274
www.Xlibris.com
Orders@Xlibris.com

65980

CONTENTS

Welcome, Y'all!

I am delighted you have decided to join me on this journey down a well-worn path of all things Southern. Whether you are Southern or not, I hope you will enjoy exploring a few of the quintessential traditions, customs, and downright hilarious aspects of our way of life south of the Mason Dixon Line.

For the past twelve years or so I have spent a good deal of my time traveling throughout the South and beyond entertaining audiences with my comedic alter ego, Maxie the Preacher's Wife. She is Southern through and through from the top of her tacky flowered hat to her red sequined shoes, an ensemble which totally reflects her persona. She loves sharing her distinctly Southern viewpoint and country take on life. In my travels, I have found that Southerners for the most part are cut from the same cloth. We love the simple things in life. Even if we're country moved to town, we still hold to down-home, traditional values. We value faith, family, friends and country. We take pride in our Southern roots, cherishing the heritage that lies behind us, and optimistically looking forward to the future before us.

If you were raised right in the South, enjoy this jaunt down memory lane, remember life at its best, and share it with a friend. If you were not raised right in the South, then you are about to immerse yourself in a world of pure d fun (see chapter 5 for an explanation of that term). Come celebrate the saga that is the South and the stories of those who were born and "raised right" in it.

Y'all have fun now, y'heah!
Rose Elaine Lumley Brantley

Acknowledgements and Dedications

This book is dedicated to all Southern women

Past, Present, and Future

But Especially to:

Ruth Smith Lumley, My mama in love and birth

Kathryn Blizzard Brantley, My mama in love and marriage

Both of whom were raised right in the South

My sisters, Mary Sue Lumley Couch and

Melinda Ruth Lumley Coghlan

Who were raised right in the South

by the same Mama as yours truly

My two daughters, Susan Kathryn Brantley Dailey and

Kati Rebecca Brantley Ayotte

Who were raised right in the South by yours truly

I hope you won't mind if I also acknowledge my baby boy,

Rickey Thomas Brantley, Jr.

Who writes soulful ballads

that make Southern women cry

A gift from being raised right in the South

Chapter 1

Raised Right in the South

*M*axie, my comedic alter ego, always begins her discourse by asking how many folks in the audience were raised right in the South. Inevitably, there are a few Yankees (an affectionate term for anyone from above the Mason Dixon Line) and sometimes even a few foreigners in the crowd. She commiserates with them over their misfortune of not being born in the South and raised right by a Southern mama. But, she always encourages them by celebrating the fact that they got here as quickly as they could.

If you are a Southern woman, you know exactly what being raised right in the South means. It means that your mama knew that good manners and proper behavior in public were as important as cornbread, collard greens, black-eyed peas and hog jowl on New Year's Day. Where *should I start? There's so much my Mama taught me that resulted in my being raised right.*

The phrases "Yes ma'am, no ma'am, yes sir, and no sir" are dead-sure give-aways that you were raised right in the South. All adults were afforded that courtesy whether they were church folks or scalawags. And we were expected to preface each name with Mr., Mrs. (pronounced Mizz or Mizzez), or Miss. To this day I still address anyone older than myself in that way. Even when invited to call an elder by his or her given name, I generally decline since I feel sure my Mama would not approve. I must say, though, that it kinda gets my goat when people just a little younger than I am call me ma'am. I simply try to remember that they are just doing what their Mama taught them.

Being raised right in the South also involves understanding the importance of faith, family, friends, and country. We were raised on the Proverbs and proverbial sayings. To this day, I sometimes get confused about which of those were Ruthisms and which were actually in the Bible. The preacher who preached my Mama's funeral quoted from some of her favorite proverbs. Her sisters said she quoted them so often when they were growing up they thought she wrote them. She might not have written them, but she surely lived by them and expected us to do the same. How blessed we were to not only hear God's Word but to see it lived out before us each day. Thank you, Mama!

To say that family is important in the South is an understatement. Who you are is determined by your lineage and knowing where you came from is of utmost consequence. The family connections do tend to get a little blurry sometimes as we consider fifth cousins ten times removed to be as close as brothers and sisters. What, you ask, are fifth cousins ten times removed? Beats me, but I know they're family. Every family in the South has its strange and unusual relatives, the ones who have eccentric tendencies and somewhat bizarre behaviors. We love them, too! In fact, one of the differences between the North and the South is that in the North they hide their crazy relatives in an upstairs closet when company comes. In the South, we bring ours downstairs and put 'em on display in the parlor so everybody can enjoy them!

And friends . . . well, let's just say that there is a fine line between friends and family in the South. There were people I called "aunt" and "uncle" all my life only to discover as an adult that we were not any blood kin at all. Not that it mattered . . . they were and are as dear as family.

Would you like to know about a Southerner's love for country? We bleed red, white, and blue! We are patriots through and through and consider it not only a duty but also an honor to serve the good old USA. We believe in the Union and stand proud with all Americans from sea to shining sea! And except for that ugly and unfortunate conflict we Southerners refer to as the War of Northern Aggression, we love all

Americans. We are obnoxiously patriotic. Our men remove their hats when Old Glory passes by. We don't even try to hide the tears when "God Bless America" is sung. And we stand proudly and belt out "The Star Spangled Banner" in our unique Southern twang. We even choke up when we hear "The Battle Hymn of the Republic" even if it was a Yankee campfire song. (Sorry, I thought I had put all that behind me!)

If arrogance wasn't one of the seven deadly sins, we would be downright haughty in our love for God and country. Whew! I feel like I need to go out and salute the flags on my front porch. In fact, I think I will. I may even burst into a rousing verse or two of "God Bless America."

Now let me make something perfectly clear before I go any further with my Southern opinion on upbringing. If you were not raised in the South, that doesn't necessarily mean that you weren't raised right. I don't mean to hurt anyone's feelings by insinuating that only Southerners were reared properly. It's what I know. It's who I am. It's how I was raised. And I believe it served me well. But if you disagree with or take offense at the opinions held by this Southern author . . . well then, you are certainly welcome to write your own book

Chapter 2

Hissy Fits, Sometimes Known as Conniption Fits

*B*eing raised right in the South means that you must never pitch a hissy fit in public. What, you say, is a "hissy fit?" If you will just elongate that first syllable and add several sss's I believe you will begin to understand. It's when the snake in you escapes and spews its poisonous venom at whoever might be standing nearby. The onset of this type fit is preceded by narrowed, flaming eyes and a furrowed brow. It can be accompanied by much writhing and flinging of hands and arms or it can take on a coiled position ready to strike at a moment's notice. It can be hazardous to your health to be too near a Southern woman pitching a "hissy fit." Now these fits can be brought on by anything from a righteous indignation over a social injustice to a broken fingernail. The results are pretty much the same. Are you getting the picture? Now *you can throw yourself all kinds of "hissy fits" in private, but a Southern lady never gives in to this primal urge in public.*

That leads us to the next indication that you have been raised right in the South. Because we were not allowed the luxury of pitching hissy fits in public, Southern matriarchs provided us with an equally effective mode of expression which lets our adversary know she has been dealt with in an appropriate manner just short of breaching the "no hissy fits in public" rule. This would be the sweet but deadly Georgia Peach "Put 'er in 'er place in no uncertain terms while still maintaining a cool, demure exterior" fit. This is most often done in a more pronounced than usual syrupy, southern drawl with a fixed steely smile. There is much gushing of endearments such as "Sugah, Honey, and Sweetie" and the profuse usage of terms such as "bless your heart" and "precious". (See chapter 3) When you are done speaking your mind, your adversary knows she has been hit by something, but she's not quite sure what. Whatever it was, she is sure she does not want to experience it again. As my Mama used to say, "Sometimes you just have to kill 'er with kindness!"

Chapter 3

Southern Greetings and Euphemisms
(Now that's a $4 word!)

*H*ave you noticed that folks in the South greet one another the same way every time? This is the standard Southern greeting, "Hi you?" which is pronounced with a flat "i". Translation: "How are you?" And the proper answer is, "Fine!" again pronounced with a flat "i". It might be important for you to understand that this is just a nicety and not an invitation to delineate all your aches and pains, cares and woes. If you are meeting someone for the first time, the next question will be, "Where you from?" It's important for Southerners to know from whence a person hails. I'm convinced this is true because we want to know if he or she is acquainted with any of our relatives who might live within fifty miles of their hailing-point. If the person greeted is a life-long friend, the next question is, "How's your mamer 'n 'em?" Translation: "How is your Mama and the rest of the family?" This is not just a nicety, but rather a genuine longing to know how each one fares and if there has been illness or tragedy since last we met. We really do care!

A uniquely Southern euphemism is the phrase "Bless your heart." I didn't know what euphemism really meant until I used it in the previous sentence and then looked it up to see if it fit. And does it ever! A euphemism is a word or phrase used in place of a term that might be considered too direct, harsh, unpleasant, or offensive. Well, the last thing we Southerners want to be is too direct, harsh, unpleasant, or offensive. Thus, the term "bless your heart" has become code for "you are so stupid!" Another Southern euphemism (I'm beginning to really like this word!) is "precious". Have you noticed that in the South everything is precious . . . the dog, the cat, the house, the dress, the husband, the children, etc. "Precious" is code for the same thing as "bless your heart". I'm telling you, when I learned what "bless your heart" and "precious" really means in the South, it freed me as a preacher's wife. I could go all over that church saying, "bless your heart" or "you're so precious", and they never knew what hit 'em . . . especially the deacons. Unfortunately, I shared this little-known secret with some church-folks one night and made one man really mad. He informed me in no uncertain terms that he was **chairman** of the deacons in his church. To which I replied, "Well, bless your heart. Then you are the most precious one of all." Sometimes people are just too precious, bless their hearts!

Another word that will distinguish we Southerners in a heartbeat is the word "y'all." FYI: "y'all" is singular and "all y'all" is plural. It slips out of our mouths like boiled okra and brands us immediately as being from south of the Mason Dixie Line. I love it! I want everybody to know I'm from the South and I'm proud of it. Several years ago, I flew to Ohio to entertain on a college campus. Because of a glitch in my schedule, I had to fly out of a different airport. I was desperately trying to explain my situation to the ticket agent so that I could change my ticket before the flight left me. He was kind and patient with this frantic soul who was ready to get back below the Mason Dixon Line. As I was leaving the counter and heading to my gate I heard him say in his best Southern accent, "Y'all come back now, y'heah!" I stopped, turned around and said, "Is it that noticeable?" He just laughed and laughed. I'm glad it is!!!

The next time you meet up with Southern friends and family, count the number of times you hear those phrases. Then bask in the sunshine of the South!

Chapter 4

Southern Mamas

*S*outhern mamas are a breed apart from all other mothers in the world. They are strong yet gentle, firm yet kind, self-sufficient yet dependent, thrifty yet extravagant, no-nonsense yet fun. They will give you just enough slack in the rope to experience a little freedom, but not enough to hang yourself. They can give you a good whoopin' and love on you all at the same time. They always have an apron to dry salty tears, wipe snotty noses, and take sweet cookies from the oven. My Mama was no exception.

She taught school for over thirty years and saw lots of things change in the educational world. She witnessed the pendulum swing from philosophy to philosophy and practice to practice, but her tried and true methods were the ones she used in her classroom. She had implemented the "no child left behind" policy long before George Bush. One thing she *insisted upon was discipline and respect. She implemented disciplinary practices that not only were good for the teacher but for her students also. By the time I came along, she had earned the respect of class after class of students. In fact, just the other day I was talking with one of her former fifth graders. She said the one thing she remembered was that Mrs. Lumley was always fair in dealing with all her students. She made sure they all toed the line. That reminded me of the day my respect for her went up a notch. We were leaving school one afternoon walking to our car. The buses were just pulling out when one little boy leaned out the window of the bus and shouted, "Bye, Old Lady Lumley!" I can only assume that he had been lulled into believing that he was safe on a moving bus and confident there was nothing she could do about his disrespect. Or perhaps he just took leave of his senses for a moment in time. Boy was he wrong! She turned around, stopped the bus, escorted him down the hall, wore his fanny out, deposited him back in his seat, waved, and shouted as his bus pulled out for a second time that day, "Have a good afternoon!" WOW! That put a healthy fear of God in me as I marveled at how she stood up for herself and every other teacher that day. Now it's a shame that what happened back then would never happen now, because I'm sure one little boy learned a valuable lesson about respect that day. Don't mess around with Mrs. Lumley or any other teacher worthy of it.*

Her insistence on discipline and respect did not end with the students. It was extended to their parents, also. She made sure she treated them with the same respect she expected in return. The Golden Rule dominated her interpersonal dealings. "Do unto others as you would have them do unto you" was the way she lived and the way she taught us to live. I overheard a phone conversation with a parent one evening. I was privy to only one side of the conversation, but I heard enough to know that she was being blasted by this irate parent for not being fair to her precious offspring. The parent must have said, "My child must get on your nerves." My Mama replied, "Honey, before the school year is out, they all get on my nerves." Southern mamas are fair and painfully honest!

My Mama also had a heart of compassion a mile wide. She has been known to leave our holiday table, load up the car with food, and take it down the street to a family who might be struggling with illness or some other undisclosed problem. Many times we daughters went along and learned valuable lessons that can't be taught from books or lectures. I've seen my Mama comfort a dear black woman after the loss of a child. The family lived in a sparsely furnished house across the tracks and it wasn't exactly the respectable place for my Mama, a middle-aged white woman, to be in the 1960's. She thought nothing of crossing cultural and racial barriers to show friendship to a woman who spent her Saturdays in our home ironing everything from my

Daddy's boxers to the pillowcases and handkerchiefs. As I look back, I realize that out-sourcing this task was the only luxury my Mama indulged in for herself. Now that I think about it, she didn't just do it for herself. She was helping someone else by providing a much-needed job in a time when opportunities were scarce for black women. She was ahead of her time when it came to friendship no matter the color of skin or the socio-economic station in life. She truly was no respecter of persons. She just did what was right, a prerequisite for being able to raise somebody right.

Mama's last years were spent locked in the dark, confused world of Alzheimer's. We gradually lost her to this terrible disease and in the end, she recognized none of us by name. Just a few days before she died we received a wonderful gift. She had spent the night experiencing one seizure after another as we helplessly watched her suffer yet another indignity caused by this awful disease. The next morning when she awoke she looked around the room, smiled, and called each of us by name. We spent the next hour or so with our Mama, the one we knew and loved, the one who tucked us in bed and kissed away our hurts, the one who put us on the straight and narrow path and expected us to stay there. At one point, the doctor came into the room and asked the same question he asked every morning, "How is she this morning?" Now this doctor had not known our Mama before the Alzheimer's. That particular morning before we could answer, she herself replied, "I'm fine, how are you?" He had to sit down for a minute. He tried to explain the change by saying that broken synapses in the brain must have temporarily re-fired or something like that. But we knew that this was a final gift from God, one last visit with our Southern Mama who raised us right.

Chapter 5

A Non-Southerner's Guide to Southernese

*B*ecause so many wonderful non-southern friends have moved South in recent years I felt it necessary to include this chapter early in the book. Maybe this will help you maneuver through the sometimes-deep waters of Southernese. This is by no means an exhaustive list, but will help you nonetheless as you live among those of us who were born and bred in the South and who cut our teeth on these colloquialisms.

Bless yer heart—*"You are so stupid."*

Yer so precious—*"You are so stupid."*

Hi you?—*"How are you?"*

Tote—*to carry*

   "Can you tote this bucket for me?"

Carry—*to transport*

   "I'll be glad to carry you to town."

How's your mamer 'n' 'em?

   "How is your Mama and the family?"

Sistah—*a flesh and blood sister; a female friend*

Bubba—*a flesh and blood brother; any Southern male*

A whoopin'—*a well-needed spanking*

Fixins—*all the trimmings of a Southern meal*

Fixin' to—*preparing to; about to*

   "I'm fixin' to go to town."

A lasko trade—*You will relay a compliment you heard about a person if*

   that person will give you a compliment first.

Yankee dime—*a kiss*

How come?—*"Why?"*

Jeet chet?—*"Did you eat yet?"*

Na chet—*"Not yet."*

Tuck another notion—*changed your mind*

   "I was fixin' to cut the grass but I tuck another notion."

So fer fer—*so far far*

   "What'd you move back so fer fer?"

Might could—*might be able to*

   "You might could move that table over there."

Ri' chere—*right here*

"I'm sure that glass was ri' chere a minute ago."

I'll swanee—*"I'll swear"*

Half a bubble off plumb—*not so bright*

"I'm afraid that poor boy is about half a bubble off plumb. Bless his heart!

It'd make you want to slap yo granny—*delicious*

"That pie was so good it'd make you wanta slap yer granny."

Pure d—*the best of the best; the purest form*

"That chocolate cake was pure d good!"

Purt 'near—*close; almost*

It's purt 'near time to go home.

You slept 'til your head got hairy—*slept a long time*

My Daddy used to say this to us when we got up in the morning.

Used to—*would—see sentence above*

Ugly as homemade sin—*very ugly*

Coyote ugly—*When you wake up after a night of partying and you are lying next to an ugly woman with your arm under her head. She is so ugly that you would rather chew your arm off and slip out quietly than wake her up.*

So ugly they had to tie a pork chop around his neck for the dogs to play with him—*very, very ugly*

Ah'm about to burn up—*"I'm very hot."*

Hot as a fat baby—*very, very hot*

Pot calling the kettle black—*accusing someone of something you are also guilty of*

Flung a cravin' on me

    "When I saw you with that biscuit and gravy, it flung a cravin' on me to have one, too."

Sho 'nuff—*absolutely*

    "Those biscuits are sho'nuff good."

Plumb—*completely*

Got off with—*embarrassed*

    "She was plumb got off with."

Slap—*all the way; completely*

    "He threw that rock slap across the river."

    "She is slap crazy!"

As slow as molasses in wintertime—*very, very slow*

As old as dirt—*very, very old*

Might would—*might*

    "I might would help you move this Saturday."

Some of my father-in-law's favorite sayings:

That boy is so slow you have to line him up with a fence post to see if he's movin'.

You knew he was lyin' 'cause his lips was movin'.

Those folks can't help being ugly, but they could stay home.

Messin' and gommin'—*nothing in particular; just messing around*

Whatcha—*what have you*

> *"Whatcha been doin'?"*

> *"Just messin' and gommin'."*

One of my Mama's favorite little poems:

> *Pretty's only skin deep*

> *But ugly's to the bone*

> *Pretty soon will fade away*

> *But ugly holds its own.*

Southern Food Items:

Grits—*This is a food made from ground corn and is best with lots of real butter*

Cathead biscuit—*a big, fluffy biscuit*

Red-eye gravy—*gravy made from ham grease and coffee (Sounds awful, but it's lip-lickin' good on a big ol' hot cathead biscuit)*

Tar biscuit *Georgia version—You poke a hole in the biscuit and fill it with syrup;*

Alabama version—You split the biscuit, put syrup on it and toast it

Soakie—*cold biscuits soaked in a cup of coffee*

My sweet friend, Cindy, who hails from Illinois, supplied me with this list of words she has found to be a problem since she came to live in Georgia.

heap of—*a lot of*

   "That surely is a heap of clothes to fold."

Pooted—*passed gas*

Tee tee—*urinated*

Young'un—*a child*

Reckon—*think*

   "I reckon I'll go on home now."

Buggy—*shopping cart*

Sack—*bag*

Home place—*the home where you grew up*

britches—*pants; backside*

   "You're gonna get your britches dirty."

   "I'm gonna tan your britches if you don't behave."

Tan—*spank*

Purdy—*pretty*

    "You're as purdy as a butterbean."

Sweet tea—*iced tea with lots of sugar*

    Southern iced tea is sweet, sweet, sweet!

Sweet milk—*not buttermilk*

Over yonder—*somewhere over there*

breakfast, dinner, supper—*morning meal, noon meal, evening meal*

Rurnt—*ruined*

    "That young'un is so spoiled he is rurnt."

    "If you leave that milk out it'll be rurnt by morning."

Coke—*all sodas*

    "What kind of coke would you like?"

Gimme—*Give me.*

Sugah—*can be the white granulated kind, but more than likely it is a kiss.*

    "Gimme some sugah."

Blistered—*sunburned*

Piddling around—*not doing much*

In a tight—*not much money*

    "We had so many bills this month we were in a tight."

Drawed up—*shrank*

    "That dress drawed up when I washed it.

To favor someone—*resemble*

    "He sure favors his daddy."

Pay no mind—*Do not pay any attention to*

Pick at—*to annoy*

  "Don't pay him no mind. He's just pickin' at you."

Running your mouth—*talking too much*

Right nice—*very nice*

Being ugly—*being mean; having a bad attitude*

  "I'm gonna tan your britches if you don't stop being ugly."

Telling a story—*lying*

Mash—*press*

  If you are a born and bred Southerner, I am sure you can think of a thousand more. Send them to me. Who knows? They might make the sequel!

Chapter 6

Sunday School Pins

If you're a Southern Baptist you don't need an explanation of the significance of the prestigious Sunday School Pin. If however, you are not so blessed, I must explain. If you had been faithful enough and/ or healthy enough to be in attendance at Sunday School every Sunday in a given quarter, you received a shiny pin—thus the term, Sunday School Pin. If you continued to have perfect attendance, you received a new and different pin every three months with other significant bars and gold leaves to hang from the previous award. Receiving a Sunday School pin was a lofty goal and one worthy of achieving. But I'm afraid I never made it more than three months due to family visits to my Papa Smith's home in Cork, Georgia and the annoyance of such stumbling blocks as viruses, colds, chicken-pox, measles, and other childhood hindrances. However, some I know persevered and displayed pins and bars and ornamental paraphernalia that trailed down their clothing for a foot or more. I can't tell you exactly what all the pins looked like, because I never got past the penny-colored three-month version. I do know that I was impressed by the splendor of all that metal and equally impressed by the perseverance that was behind each hard-earned medal. I secretly longed for the privilege of being one of the few, the proud, the Sunday School Pin crowd. But, alas, every armor (or Sunday School pin) has its chink. Some of the Sunday School Pin crowd have been known to drag themselves from their sickbeds, show up at Sunday School, fill out the perfunctory attendance card, and then drag themselves back to their respective sickbeds. Rural legend has it that some even checked out of the hospital just long enough to be counted present and then retreated to the sterile environment of said hospital. That concerned me a bit. Was a Sunday School Pin important enough to jeopardize your health and contaminate everybody at church that morning? Evidently, it was! I guess all's fair in love and awards!

Chapter 7

The Sunday Morning Hustle

*I*t never ceased to amaze me that I could get up at 6:00 AM Monday through Friday, feed and dress a family of five, and get us all out the door by 7:30 for school and work. But let Sunday roll around and for the life of me I couldn't get us all up and going and out the door in time for Sunday School at 10:00 AM. What is that all about? Most of the time I blamed it on the fact that Satan just didn't want us to make it or he wanted us to be downright ornery by the time we did. I hate to admit it, but he usually won.

This disruption of a perfectly good Sunday morning routine has been around for a long time. I can remember Sunday mornings growing up. We only had one bathroom (at least it was inside) for five people with four of them being female. It was a mad dash to be the first one in the bathroom and usually there were at least two standing outside yelling *for the other one to hurry. When we finally got in the car with barely enough time for the five-minute ride to church, we realized that someone was missing . . . Daddy. We fussed and fumed that we would be late. We never could figure out why he was always the last one in the car on Sunday morning. Duh . . . he always had to wait for three daughters and one wife to get out of the bathroom. When he finally did get in the car, he would light up that King Edward cigar and just about cause a family feud before we got to church. Nobody wanted to smell like King Edward when we going to worship the King of Kings. I think that was payback for hogging (taking too much time) the bathroom.*

Things didn't change much when our own children were growing up. Even with two bathrooms there was still a mad dash to get there first. And there were still two other children waiting not so patiently for the third to get out. When they were little, it seemed that when I would get one dressed the other two had lost a shoe or a sock. I began to dress one, sit that one on the sofa, and dare him to move until I could dress the next one. That worked okay for one on the sofa, but when two got there, it was playtime. This harem-scarem routine became known as the Sunday Morning Hustle. It went something like this:

The Sunday Morning Hustle

We got up Sunday morning with no time left to spare,

No one can seem to find socks and shoes;

There are just no patching pairs.

I burned the toast and realized

The milk's no good, it's sour.

It's almost time for Sunday School,

We've got less than an hour.

The preacher's sermon has just become

breakfast for the doggy,

The dryer's quit, I just found out

my Sunday dress is soggy.

There's just no other option,

I'll have to wear last Sunday's clothes.

Oh, no! I've just discovered I've got runners in my hose.

The kids are dressed, I've banished them to wait out in the car

I've found a pair of pantyhose whose runs don't go too far.

Well, now we're in the car and we're looking pretty good

When thick black smoke begins to pour

out from under the hood.

We've finally made it to the church we're all a little riled;

I've fussed and fumed and carried on

about the morning's trials.

But when we step out of the car you won't believe your eyes,

We're the perfect preacher's family complete with Baptist smiles.

Chorus:

Do the Sunday morning hustle,

You'd better hurry along.

Do the Sunday morning hustle,

When everything goes wrong.

Sunday morning in the preacher's house

Makes you want to swear and curse.

Sunday morning in the preacher's house

Is just like yours (but worse!)

Chapter 8

Let's All Go Down to the River

*M*ost small churches in the South could not afford baptismal pools so they did their baptizin' in the nearest river or creek. You could join the church anytime during the year, but unless you were fond of icy water, you wanted to wait until at least spring to be baptized . . . preferably summer. Baptizin' Day was a grand and glorious affair. Those who had been saved throughout the year had been awaiting this day with much anticipation. Church would convene on the banks of the nearest body of water suitable for baptizin'. Now before the actual baptismal could begin the deacons would clear the waters of snakes and turtles and other undesirables. Sometimes these included sunbathers and swimmers who would rather commune with God in nature instead of going to church like their mamas raised them. When the baptismal area was clear, the preacher would wade out into the *water until he found the correct baptizin'-depth. On one occasion, my preacher-husband was not aware of a sharp drop-off and found himself swimming until he could get his footing again. Now that was a dignified sight. Usually a baptizin' assistant would accompany the preacher. His job was to look out for snakes that chose to reclaim their territory before the baptizin' was done. The congregation would sing an appropriate hymn, usually "Shall We Gather At the River". Then each baptismal candidate would step into the water, go down a wet sinner, and come up a shoutin' saint! It was impressive! After a rousing rendition of "When We All Get to Heaven" a satisfied group of church-folks would head home and leave those sacred waters to the snakes and swimmers until the next baptizin' day.*

There were some folks who didn't want to wait for warmer weather so on those rare occasions we would use the baptistery at the church in town. On one such cold winter Sunday, the heater in the pool was not working and the water was ice-cold. The middle-aged candidate for baptism was already afraid of water and was not anticipating this event with great joy. When she found there was no warm water, she was even more skeptical about this baptizin' thing. My preacher-husband waded into the water and did everything he could not to scream when that cold water hit his middle. The candidate was finally coaxed into the freezing water and the two stood with teeth chattering trying to make this as painless as possible. Both had become somewhat acclimated to the cold from the waist down, but when the preacher tried to take her under the water, all heaven broke loose! She started flinging her arms and let go with a blood-curdling shriek as she knocked off the "In Memory of" flowers on the edge of the baptistery. Kicking and screaming she was baptized that day in a service neither she nor any of us will ever forget. Amidst half-stifled giggles, we headed home that day leaving those sacred frigid waters to some other unsuspecting baptizin' crowd.

Chapter 9

Southern Comfort

*F*ood! It's at the heart of all that is Southern. We love food so much down here that even our endearing names for one another have something to do with food: Honey, Sugah, Sweetie Pie, Dumpling, Tater, Punkin, etc. We're all about comfort food and the more butter the better. Good Southern mamas will push groceries on you like a backstreet drug dealer pushing heroin and sometimes with less finesse. They are not above using bribery and even guilt to persuade you to have just one more helping. According to them, it would be an insult to turn down a second or third piece of pie. How many mamas do you know who have not used this line when encouraging a young'un to eat? "Think of all the starving children in the world who would love to have what's on your plate!" I'll admit it, that phrase has guilted me more than once to try to clean my plate. The truth is that over the years we have been bribed and *guilted into obesity in the South. That reminds me of that cartoon of the sheep, "Ewe's not fluffy, ewe's stuffy."*

Enough of that depressing talk. They say you are what you eat. If I am what I eat, then I am fast, cheap, and easy unless I am at church.

In the Baptist church we meet and eat, and rarely do we do one without the other. We have fellowship dinners, covered-dish suppers, coffees, teas, showers with dainty finger foods, prayer breakfasts, soup and salad luncheons, socials, and the most famous of all, dinner on the ground. Every year at the same time we have what we call Homecoming. That's when we invite all our friends and family to come back home for a day of worship and eating. It's like a big ole church reunion! The highlight of the day is dinner on the ground. Now, we don't literally put the food on the ground, although they might have in days gone by. They certainly might have eaten on the ground, picnic-style. Today we put the food on tables in the Fellowship Hall and eat in the cool comfort of air-conditioned buildings. But I remember a time when we actually did eat outside, gnats and all. There would be table after table loaded with all the covered dishes the ladies of the church had prepared. There was fried chicken and ham, fresh vegetables, dinner rolls, biscuits, cornbread (fried and pone), congealed salads of all kinds, and desserts. Oh, the desserts!!! There was every sort of cake and pie imaginable, cookies, fruit tarts, and my Mama's specialty, peach cobbler. I can still smell Homecoming! There were galvanized tubs of sweet tea and lemonade floating in crushed ice.

And no, we didn't get any kind of lead poisoning. In fact, the metal of the tubs probably enhanced the flavor. It was a grand time of fellowshipping with one another and eating until you couldn't hold another bite.

The story is told of a little Baptist boy who came home from school one day and told his mama that the teacher wanted everyone to bring a symbol of their religious faith the next day for Show and Share. (That was before all this political correctness hogwash!) She sent him to school the next day, religious symbol in hand. When it was time to share, the first little boy said, "My name is Christopher. I'm a Catholic and these are rosary beads." The next child stood and said, "My name is Samuel, I'm Jewish and this is a Star of David." The little Baptist boy stood to his feet and said, "My name is Rick. I'm a Southern Baptist and this is a covered-dish." If the shoe fits . . .

Baptist preachers are known for their ability to hold their own around the dinner table. One such preacher had eaten so much fried chicken his wife was plumb embarrassed. At the end of the meal, the farmer-host's rooster hopped up on the windowsill and began to crow loudly. The preacher commented on what a proud rooster he was. The farmer replied, "He should be proud, he just had three sons to enter the ministry!"

My preacher-husband has misinterpreted some Scripture in the Bible. The Bible says your body is a temple. Well, he's trying to make a cathedral out of his. Before you laugh too hard, you'd better check and see if you have a building project going on. Why, just this week I had a call at the church. A man said, "I want to talk to the head hog at the *trough!" I told him that if he wanted to talk to my preacher-husband he'd have to call him something respectable like Dr. or Reverend or Brother. He said, "Lady, I didn't mean to offend you. I just called to tell you I wanted to give $10,000 to your church." I said, "Hang on a minute; I believe the Big Pig just walked in!"*

(I'll let you decide if those stories are truth-telling or just preaching!)

I find comfort in the belief that our love for food is a biblical concept. After all, the Bible promises that one day we will sit down with Jesus at the Marriage Supper of the Lamb! Just think, the all-you-can-eat buffet to end all all-you-can-eat buffets. All the chocolate you can eat, all the sweets you can eat, all the spicy food you can eat . . . NO CALORIES and NO HEARTBURN! Praise God from whom all gravy flows!

Mama's Peach Cobbler

3 c. fresh peaches

1 c. sugar

1 c. flour

1 c. milk

1 stick butter

Peel and slice fresh peaches; set aside. Mix sugar and flour; add milk and set aside. Melt butter in baking dish. Pour the milk, sugar and flour mixture in the butter. Do not stir. Place peaches on mixture. Do not stir. Bake in 350 degree preheated oven for about 1 hour.

Serve warm with homemade ice cream! It don't get no better than this! (A Southern phrase that says it all!)

Chapter 10

Southern Weddings

*B*y the time I was a senior in college I had sung or played at almost a hundred Southern weddings and I have an armful of bangle bracelets to prove it. (That seemed to be the gift of choice for musicians back then.) As a Pastor's wife, I directed and attended many, many more so I consider myself an expert on the subject. Now southern weddings are as varied as the couples hitched. I've been to fancy church weddings, back-to-nature nuptials where bees nearly carried away the attendees, and Harley Davidson affairs with classic Harleys marking the bridal aisle. The bride, arrayed in white leather, proceeded to her black leather clad groom down that shiny, chrome aisle. I have hosted small home ceremonies where there was only the couple, the preacher and myself. I've heard of romantic beach weddings, little mountain chapel weddings, even nuptials of couples as they hurled themselves *toward earth after jumping from airplanes. Now that gives a whole new meaning to the phrase "till death do us part." Whatever the place, the time, or the surroundings there are some elements that set Southern weddings apart from all the rest.*

The bride's dress is always white or some shade of that elusive trademark of purity and chastity. Never mind that her past might be littered with innuendoes and gossip, or outright—caught-redhanded evidence. And never mind that her attendants are her four children by four different daddies. And never mind that the precious little ring bearer and flower girl are actually products of the union about to be nuptialized. (That's not a real word, you say. Well it is now!) And never mind that she and the dashing bridegroom set up housekeeping years ago. Even if all this is true, the dress still must be white or some shade of that elusive trademark of purity and chastity. My hometown still holds to traditional values. When a couples' first baby comes along, whether they've been married eight months or eight years, you can be assured somebody's still counting. Call me old-fashioned but I still love to go to a wedding where there are no innuendoes, gossip or red-handed evidence. It makes me feel like there is still hope in this crazy world.

The groom still wears black, be it leather, tuxedo, suit, or t-shirt and jeans. His apparel is still black. A child asked her mama, "Why does the bride always wear white?" The mother replied, "Because this is the happiest day of her life!" The child then asked, "Then why does the groom wear black?" Hmmm! Such a wise question from one so young. I have some observations regarding the black attire. Perhaps it is because black tuxedoes are the cheapest to rent, black suits are the easiest to find, black t-shirts and jeans are reminiscent of Johnny Cash, and well everybody knows that all bikers wear black. Perhaps, the black attire helps to distinguish the bridegroom from the bride. And maybe in some cases he actually is in mourning. I've known of more than one bridegroom who has been encouraged by a gun-totin' papa-in-law-to-be to show up and stand up. Remember, we're talking about Southern weddings.

The Southern church reception generally consists of wedding cake, green or pink fruit punch, nuts and mints. But I must say, weddings these days are becoming much more involved. I've been to some weddings lately that would put the Homecoming spread to shame. I'm afraid we've become entangled in that "my-daughter's-wedding-was-better-than-your-daughter's-wedding" syndrome. And to be perfectly honest, my oldest daughter's wedding was somewhat of a fancy affair with the spread becoming more elaborate than any of us imagined. But, it was a wonderful event and well worth all the compliments on the food and decor. Okay, okay . . . I was temporarily affected by the malady, too. When the second daughter decided to marry, she chose a much simpler course. She married at a quaint little depot in the heart of town. Because her Mainer fiancé and his family would be visiting the South for the first time, she chose to introduce them to real Southern foods instead of the traditional wedding grub. There was lemonade served with old-fashioned dippers, assorted sandwiches, fresh fruit including watermelon of course, the obligatory cake, nuts and mints, and finally boiled peanuts. Not many of our Northern guests thought that soggy peanuts was a good idea. However, both weddings were wonderful and in the words of our hometown newspaper at the end of every social event piece, "A good time was had by all."

One couple I know thought it would be a good idea to get married after Sunday church and ask everybody to bring a covered dish for the reception. I wish I had thought of that!

The preacher still officiates at the ceremony. And believe me, my preacher-husband has officiated at his share. Weddings are not his favorite part of the ministry. In fact, he says he would much rather preach a funeral than officiate a wedding. Reason one, everybody is too upset and grieved at a funeral to be offended if he doesn't do everything just perfectly. Reason two, the main participant at a funeral won't gripe about the service. And reason three, there's no mother-of-the-bride (MOTB) at a funeral. At a recent wedding, the groom came up to the preacher after the ceremony and said those words every preacher loves to hear, "How much do I owe you, Preacher?" With the bride standing nearby the preacher replied, "Why don't you pay me according to the beauty of your bride?" The groom reached in his wallet and gave the preacher two dollar bills. The preacher lifted up the veil, took a look at the bride and gave the young groom a dollar back. Now that'll get a U-Haul backed up to your parsonage door in no time flat. I guess he forgot about the MOTB.

Chapter 11

Southern Funerals

*S*outhern funerals are as sorrowful as Southern weddings are joyful. Southerners have great difficulty saying good-by to family and friends when parted by death. And again, Southern funerals have certain trademarks like no other.

Black is the color of choice for Southern funerals. It would be an atrocious faux pas to show up at a funeral in sunshine yellow, fire-engine red, or any other bold cheerful color. Why, it would be as if you were glad the dearly departed was departed. Every self-respecting Southern woman has a funeral dress, one that is always ready in case of the unexpected. An acquaintance told about the time she wore a frog-print dress to a funeral. (I just heard a gasp from Southern Mamas living and dead!) To make matters worse, this friend realized as she sat in the church that the dress also had the word, "CROAK" written all over *it! That dress certainly was not appropriate for a Southern funeral. And everybody knows you never wear a new dress to a funeral. There's something about it being bad luck. Tell me, how much worse could your luck get? You're already having to get out the funeral dress! And many Southern women go to great lengths to make sure that should it be their time, their families know exactly what they should be laid out in, who should do their hair, and what jewelry should be buried with them. Proud to the everlasting! I heard someone muse, "Do you have to spend eternity in the clothes you were buried in?" If that's true, heaven is going to an interesting place!*

A wake becomes another opportunity for Southerners to eat. At the first sign that a dearly departed has departed, the food begins to pour in. Casseroles, cakes, pies, and especially potato salad fill refrigerators. Sound strange? Not really, remember we are big on comfort food. Can you think of any other occasion when you would need more comfort than at the funeral time? I heard Ken Davis, a noted Christian comedian, tell this story of the funeral potato salad. He said that he would laugh and tell his audiences how Southerners always brought potato salad when there was a death in the family. It was a long-standing Southern tradition. Several days after burying his precious little grandson, his wife opened their refrigerator door and burst into tears. When he came to her side all she could say was, "Look, potato salad!"

The amount of food and the number of friends is synonymous . . . the more food, the more friends and vice versa. When we moved to Dallas, Texas I found things to be quite different from back home in Georgia. Or it could have just been the difference between the big city and a small country town. We lived in a crowded residential section of Dallas and did not know any of our neighbors except for a sweet little old lady next door. When we found out days after her passing that she had gone to be with the Lord, I remember thinking, "Todo, we're not in Kansas any more." No friends visited her home, no one brought potato salad, and no one sat up through the night and reminisced about the dearly departed. My prayer was, "Lord, don't let me die out here."

Sitting up with the dead is another tradition in the South. Friends and family would gather and spend the night reminiscing and remembering the recently dearly departed. There were tears and laughter, sighs and smiles, and always lots of food to help you make it through the night. My Mama carried this tradition a little too far. My Daddy worked at the local funeral home and drove the ambulance for emergency runs to the hospital. One evening after he had picked up the ashes of a recently dearly departed from the crematorium, he came by the house for a bite to eat. Before he could finish eating, he received an emergency ambulance call and had to leave the ashes of the dearly departed at our home. When I got home from my date later that evening, I found my Mama sitting quietly in the living room. I queried, "Mama, why are you still up?" She replied, "This poor man didn't have anyone to sit up with him tonight, so I did." There on the coffee table was an urn with the dearly departed inside. It was a bit unnerving to know that this dearly departed would not be departing until the next morning. Oh well, at least he had my Mama to do the right thing by him.

If you could play and/or sing, you were frequently called upon to supply the music for funerals around town. Fortunately, for my Daddy he had three daughters who could play and sing and play and sing we did. Even today, I probably spend an inordinate amount of time providing the music for funerals of folks I know and love, and folks I've never met before. My sister whose husband was an undertaker spent more time than I did at funerals. Bless her heart!

Two old-time funeral favorites are Precious Memories and Just One Rose Will Do, two of the saddest songs you'll ever want to hear. I always felt like a bit of a hypocrite standing among a ton of wreaths and sprays singing, "Just One Rose Will Do." And "Precious Memories" . . . that one will rip the hardest heart out of a soul. A dear friend of mine loves that song and I think of him every time I sing it! That's the only way I can keep from losing it. This one's always for you, Ken!

My daddy tells of a family who found themselves in the position of having to funeralize one of their own. They were not sure of proper funeral etiquette and asked him before the funeral, "When would be the best time to cry?" To which he replied, "Well, probably the best time *would be during the songs." And boy did they take his advice. On the first note of the each song, they let loose with some of the most mournful wailing you've ever heard. At the end of each song, it was as silent as a tomb. Now that is following proper Southern etiquette to a T.*

Chapter 12

Vacation Bible School

*W*hen I was growing up, the highlight of the summer was Vacation Bible School. We looked forward to VBS with great expectancy. In our small town the Baptist Church, the Methodist Church, and the Christian Church usually had VBS the same week. On Saturday before the big event we all had a simultaneous kick-off with games, refreshments (remember we have to eat every time we meet!) and a big VBS Parade. Each church group of VBS'ers converged on the square with banners and signs touting the beginning of the biggest summer event in town. Our arrival was heralded by the big red Fire Truck with sirens and horns screaming! We proudly marched around the courthouse square unashamedly proclaiming that the next week we would be studying THE BIBLE and learning more about JESUS and possibly even committing the rest of our lives to the MISSION FIELD or

FULL-TIME MINISTRY! Can you imagine what would have happened if today's politically correct police had been standing on the street corner that day! Why there wouldn't have been enough smelling salts in the drug store to revive them! Now those were the Good Old Days!

There were a few years the churches forgot to coordinate VBS week. That meant we could go to each VBS and we loved it! In fact, I'd have gladly been sprinkled just to go to the Methodist VBS. Our mamas loved it, too . . . three weeks of VBS. Summer bliss! When my children were coming along, I scouted out potential Vacation Bible Schools as early as May so as not to pass up an opportunity to make sure they were properly schooled.

For an entire week, we heard Bible Stories, dressed as Biblical characters and acted out our own versions of those stories. We sang about Jesus and poured our little hearts out in simple and sincere prayers. That week we loved Jesus with all our being and knew without a doubt that He loved us even more! With child-like faith many of us began our lifelong walk with this wonderful Savior. Some even made that noble choice to follow Jesus in some kind of full-time ministry (that's the kind you get paid for). Our young lives were changed forever!

There were all kinds of crafts. We made macaroni-embossed cigar-box jewelry holders spray-painted gold. We spent hours on roosters made from all kinds of seeds and shellacked to last a lifetime. However, I couldn't tell you where mine is now. I think something ate the seeds. There were popsicle-stick birdhouses, beaded cross necklaces, finger-painted masterpieces, Plaster of Paris handprints, and more! There was enough glue, spray paint, and shellac to furnish the entire town with a high. I'm sure there must have been a fog hanging over the church that week. How proud we were of our VBS art!

And the refreshments . . . nothing was better on a hot summer VBS day than watered-down red Kool-Aid and homemade cookies. Sometimes we were treated to popsicles and ice cream. And, on the last day of VBS week, there were always hotdogs, chips, and drinks. Those VBS delicacies were as good as dinner-on-the-ground vittles to us.

On the post-VBS Sunday evening, our friends and family joined us for the Commencement Service. We proudly stood and sang our VBS songs with gusto. We pledged our allegiance to the American flag, the Christian flag and the Bible and displayed our newfound knowledge of Scripture by reciting the books of the Bible and memory verses we had learned. We basked in the applause and the accolades and knew without a doubt that God was smiling, too!

Of all my VBS experiences, two of them taught me truths I'll never forget. At the end of VBS one year we were enjoying a picnic at the local camp when word came that our dear friend and neighbor of only twelve years of age had perished in a trucking accident. We were devastated and rushed to the side of our neighbors to walk with them down this dark, lonesome road. Even as a little child, I felt their pain and heartache and

I saw the depth of Southern compassion. Food and friendship flowed in and out of that home like water in the taps. How glad I was that friends were like family.

The second experience would also end terribly as two little boys would hop on a bike for a quick ride before VBS began that morning. Tragically, a truck hit them and both were severely injured. Sadly, Little Mark died from his injuries. In a split second, one of our own was taken! I found it very difficult to understand how this could happen to someone so young. I remember watching his grieving parents and big brother struggle to cope with such heart-wrenching sorrow. Our VBS teachers struggled along with us that week to discover this great truth: God is good . . . all the time and all the time . . . God is good! Circumstances may stink, but God is always good!

Life Lessons Learned at Vacation Bible School:

1) *Hiding God's Word in your heart will last you all the days of your life.*

2) *Roosters made of seeds will fade away, but the Biblical seeds planted in your heart will grow and prosper you all the days of your life.*

3) *Red Kool-Aid will leave you thirsty, but the Water of Life that Jesus gives will quench your spiritual thirst all the days of your life.*

4) *And even when life tragically ends, Jesus will carry you home with Him for all the days of your eternal life forevermore.*

Chapter 13

Summer Delicacies

*W*e didn't have any fast food joints or big chain restaurants in our little town. What we did have was the soda fountain at the local drug store. Mmmm, I can still taste the cherry cokes, scoop ice cream, and ice cream floats served in real glass soda fountain containers. What a treat to sit on those stools at the soda fountain bar and feel like you had arrived.

Those were delicious, but my favorite summer delicacy was then, and is now, ice-cold watermelon. It must have been heaven to be so blessed as to live on a farm where you could grow your own watermelons. Can you just imagine being able to go straight to the source and eat all the watermelon you could hold? Now, that's what I call being in Hog Heaven. Sadly, we were not so fortunate. We had to buy our watermelons from the icehouse. What, you say, is an icehouse? Simple. It was the place

where you bought ice, big chunks of the stuff as in fifty-pound blocks.
And they also sold watermelons, ice-cold ones at that. What else would
you expect from the icehouse? It was a grand occasion when my Daddy
would bring home a huge, sweet melon fresh from the icehouse. Friends
and relatives came out of nowhere. No problem. Those huge melons
could feed a crowd. We ate until our bellies were as big as watermelons.
We had seed spitting contests. We dripped that sweet nectar down the
front of our clothes with no thought of a napkin. In other words, we
partied down Southern-style! When there was nothing left but the rind,
my Mama took those and made watermelon rind preserves, one of my
Daddy's favorites. In fact, as I look back that's probably why we had
watermelon so often. To think, my own Daddy had ulterior motives. We
thought he just loved us that much!

When we weren't enjoying summer melons we were cranking out
homemade ice cream. And I do mean cranking out! This was before
the electric version and it took the whole crowd to produce that frozen
dessert. Everybody took a turn at the crank. Round and round it went
until the liquid became thick, sweet ice cream. Breyers didn't have
anything on us back then. Sometimes we added strawberries or peaches,
but the best was the plain old vanilla. Once again, the sound of that
churn brought friends and relatives running with spoon and bowl in
hand. As far as we were concerned, it didn't get any better than that! I
miss those good old days when the watermelon and ice cream flowed

freely and family and friends slowed down long enough to enjoy them. Oh well, I guess I'll just have to drown my sorrows with a big slice of watermelon and chase it with a bowl of homemade ice cream. That'll work!

Chapter 14

Snakes, Gnats, and Lightning Bugs

For some reason people from up north, affectionately known as Yankees, seem to think that the South is overrun by snakes, especially the dreaded rattlesnake. Never mind that my eighty-four-year-old mother-in-law usually kills one or two every year on her farm and that she is even now recovering from a rattle-snake bite, the first in her eighty-four years. In fact, she just bought a new hoe so that she would be able to keep the rattlesnake population manageable this summer. And never mind that just last week I saw a dead one in the road (the only good kind of rattlesnake) and I found an unidentifiable snakeskin in my back yard. But other than that, I can't imagine where city-folks get their information.

My country-raised husband has some very interesting snake stories from his youth on the farm. There was the time when he was in the cotton field and a rattler hung his fang in his tennis shoe. He kicked that shoe, rattler and all, as far as he could kick. He says that to this day, even after plowing that field year after year, shoe nor rattlesnake have been seen since.

Sitting in church one Sunday morning listening to her Daddy tell one of his famous snake stories, our daughter Kati looked up at me and said, "Is he telling the truth or is he just preaching?" What a wise question from one so young! Don't believe everything you hear about snakes in the South, but do be careful where you step on a hot, humid summer day!

Gnats . . . the g is silent, but the gnat is not. That constant buzzing and what appears to be flying black pepper all around your face is a positive indication that gnat season is upon us. You can't get away from them so don't even waste your time trying. Just accept them as God's curse and move on. On a sizzling, muggy, summer day, you will find yourself swatting them from your eyes, blowing them out your nose, and spitting them out of your mouth . . . unless of course you have gum and then you just keep on chewing. Much of our protein during the summer months comes from the gnats consumed on a given day. My Daddy used to say that you could tell a local from a foreigner by the way he dealt with gnats. A foreigner would wear himself out swatting those pesky little devils and a local would simply blow them away with a quick blast of air from the corner of his mouth. There is very definitely a gnat line in Georgia which the gnats will not cross. Above the gnat line . . . no gnats. Below the line . . . hordes of them! I was very fortunate to live above the gnat line for a number of years. Recently we felt the urge to move back home to be close to our first grandson. In all the excitement of coming back home, I forgot about the gnats. Oh well, a few gnats won't be a deal-breaker . . . or will they?

If you live in the city with plenty of streetlights and neon signs, then you don't have any idea how dark it can be in the country where those don't exist. If you've never seen a country night sky far from the artificial light of the city, you have missed one of God's great light shows. The brilliance of stars millions of miles away attests to the fact that God is an awesome God. This magnificent display of His majesty will take your breath away. A sight not quite so majestic but equally as magnificent is the lightning bug, or firefly, if you prefer. I spent many summer evenings chasing, catching and bottling lightning bugs. You see, if you put them in a jar you could carry that little light with you. Don't get your PETA panties in a wad. We always let them go. I was fascinated by the unexplainable little taillight that blinked off and on as they flew through the night. Now someone much smarter than I has tried to enlighten me as to the scientific reasoning for that little light, but for the life of me it did not compute. I rather enjoy being oblivious to the science of that light and just revel in the fact that God's creation is so intricate and involved that He gave a little bitty insect a blinking rear-end that has intrigued many a child for thousands of years. Ah, ignorance is bliss, after all!

Chapter 15

Front Porch Visiting and Back Door Calling

*T*he front porch was for sitting on warm summer evenings watching those lightning bugs light up the night with their mini-fireworks exhibition. It was base for playing "Tag" and home for playing "Ain't No Boogers Out Tonight." That game used to scare the willies out of me, but I loved every minute of it. It was the place where I sat with my Papa Dude on many Friday nights watching and waiting for my Daddy to come home from his job as a traveling insurance salesman. It was where we shelled peas and butterbeans on summer afternoons, read books, played games, and enjoyed a thunderstorm or two. It was where we talked and visited, reminisced and remembered, sang and joked, discussed politics and religion, and generally enjoyed each other's company.

It was the place to sit with a beau and steal a kiss. It was also the place where my Mama turned the lights on and off to remind a reluctant suitor it was time to go home. With three daughters, I wonder how many times that switch had to be replaced.

I love front porches! It is the first place I furnished in our century old renovated farmhouse. It is my favorite living space with its white wicker rockers, antique chaise lounge, and much-loved porch swing. It is the place my little Levi and I swing, sing and take a little nap some mornings. Not much has changed when it comes to front porches in the South, except that we don't spend enough time there anymore.

The front door was rarely used as it generally led to the living room or parlor which was only used on the Sunday it was your turn to feed the preacher (see the next chapter), for receiving guests when there was a death in the family, or for the occasional door-to-door salesman who didn't know any better. Other than that, it was wasted space. One friend was lamenting the fact that her living room was useless, only to be reminded by her granddaughter, whose mother had been married on more than one occasion, that she simply had to have a living room if for nothing but her mother's weddings.

The back door was for calling. It's where friends and family called and more times than not, walked right on in preceded by a proper, "Yoohoo!" Living in a church parsonage had its own unique problems when it came to back doors. We had some parishioners who took the communistic approach, "what's yours is mine," and made themselves right at home, invited or not. I remember one such gentleman who came right on in, and asked where "our" glasses were. I sweetly told him that "my" glasses were in that cabinet. I wanted to say, "They may be "your" cabinets, but they're "my" glasses. However, I'm too much of a Southern lady to stoop to that kind of banter. Bless his heart!

The reason Southerners liked to use back doors is that they usually led right to the kitchen, the heart of the home. It's where they knew some kind of goody would be waiting for them. A glass of iced-tea, a cup of freshly brewed coffee, a slice of homemade cake or pie, a plate of apple tarts, or a batch of hot-out-of-the-oven cookies could almost always be found within those walls. Another commodity in abundance would be the friendly face of a neighbor and friend ready and willing to lend a listening ear. I think I miss that more than anything. Well, I guess it's up to me to make sure that there is still one back door and one kitchen that remains open for neighborhood business. It might be tea or coffee, the decaffeinated kind, and probably some semi-homemade pastry instead of the homemade variety, but the friendly face of a neighbor and friend will still be available to lend a listening ear. Y'all come on in!

Chapter 16

Feeding the Preacher

*I*n the South, dinner is the noon meal and supper is the evening meal. Breakfast is still breakfast except it is very early and consists of things like grits, red-eye gravy, cathead biscuits, cured ham sliced fresh, link sausage that was hanging in the smokehouse just minutes before, and dark, thick, sweet, cane syrup. You can't beat that! Ooh, I just made myself hungry!

Recently, my Maine-born-and-bred son-in-law, Lew, was trying to decide where he wanted to go for his evening birthday meal. The first place he chose was an Italian restaurant which unfortunately was closed that evening. His next choice was a country-cooking, all-you-can-eat-till-you-bust restaurant. We all agreed this would be a good place, but when our oldest daughter relayed this info to her husband, he told her it wasn't open in the evening. When I told Lew he said, "But I called *them and they said they were serving dinner." Then a knowing look came over him and he said, "It's the "dinner" thing, isn't it?" He's still learning Southernese.*

Whatever you call that meal right after Sunday morning services, it became one of two dirty jobs for parishioners of small country churches . . . feeding the preacher. The other job was cleaning the church. And so to make it easy to remember, the week it was your turn to clean the church you also had to take the preacher and his family home for Sunday dinner (that's at noon, remember). Now most members were very gracious and really put on the dog (not literally) that day. We dined sumptuously on fresh vegetables (in season and out), fresh meat, homemade from scratch cakes and pies, fresh-baked biscuits and cornbread, sweet tea and/or lemonade. No wonder my husband went from a fit 130 pounds to a . . . well, let's just say the beginnings of his diabetes probably started at some of those tables.

I remember one family we visited regularly on this rotating schedule. They raised rabbits. Now I have never been able to eat rabbit because of this recurring vision of Bugs Bunny munching on a carrot repeating, "What's up, Doc?" We always asked the Daddy of the family, "What are we having for dinner?" And his response was always the same, "Goat-nose and okra!" I knew that was a joke, but I wasn't too sure of the rabbit thing. He always hinted that one Sunday they might just be serving rabbit. I always made sure I detoured by the rabbit hutches to count them before going in the house for lunch (oops, I mean dinner!). They loved to pull this town-girl's leg and probably got a bigger kick out of my naïveté of **counting** *the rabbits from month to month.*

Eating with parishioners was always an adventure. My preacher-husband found himself seated at a lavish country spread one evening. You name it, they had it. But the centerpiece of the meal was a large plate of fried pork chops. That is what he calls finger food today. As the dinner progressed, the pork chops began to decrease in number until there was only one lone chop left. He forked that remaining portion of pig and the family's little boy began to cry and shout, "Mama, that man got my pork chop!" Awkward, huh! Maybe so, but it was great material for a Maxie song by the same name, "Mama, That Man Got My Pork Chop!" God works in mysterious ways.

I've been on the giving end and the receiving end of feeding the preacher. I can only recall a few times growing up when we actually entertained the preacher in our home, but one is especially vivid. Our dining room set was already an antique by the time I came along and was a bit wobbly from much use. One chair was especially lame with one leg on its last. We had been coached and warned that whatever we did we were not to let the preacher sit in that chair. I don't know how it happened, probably the providence of God, but that is the very chair he chose. I know my Mama was horrified and probably did some of her finest praying throughout that meal. Now Brother Smith was a gifted storyteller and we spent the entire meal being entertained by his colorful anecdotes of his days as an undertaker in the hills of Tennessee. One story was about how he found himself in the awkward position of having to catch an overzealous, over-sized mourner as she "fell out" at the viewing. Mimicking her movements, he leaned back in that crippled chair and the thing fell all to pieces leaving him in a pile on the dining room floor. We knew better than to laugh at the funniest sight we had ever seen in that dining room. However, the look on my Mama's face was crystal clear. Laugh and die! It wasn't until Brother Smith looked up from the floor and said, "Go ahead and laugh!" that we almost fell out of our own chairs in sidesplitting guffaws. Even Mama laughed!

Chapter 17

Easter Clothes

*E*aster is a splendid time of celebration in the South. The arrival of spring and the anticipation of new Easter clothes encouraged Southern ladies, young and old, to shake off the doldrums of winter and wake up to the fresh rebirth of spring. Wasn't God right on target when He scheduled the Resurrection to coincide with Easter and Spring?

We didn't do the Easter Bunny thing, but Mama always made sure we had new Easter clothes. The dresses were usually homemade which we thought was wonderful because our Mama was a gifted seamstress. We spent hours in the fabric store perusing the aisles of colorful material which would soon become Easter frocks. We drooled over lace and buttons which would add just the right finishing touch. Sometimes Mama didn't even need a pattern. She could make revisions, add details, and fit her creations to exactly the shape and size we happened to be at *the time, creatively giving each of us a one-of-a-kind designer outfit. We awoke many mornings to the sound of that old Singer sewing machine whirring out Designs by Ruth. The dress might have been homemade, but the accessories were store-bought. They included a hat, gloves, frilly socks, white or black patent shoes, and a pocketbook to match. My Daddy tells of one such Easter when I arrived at church with every accessory in place, but by the end of the service he was carrying the hat and purse. As we left the church that morning, he passed the proprietor of the local Five and Dime Store and said, "Here, you can have this hat and purse back. We're done with them."*

My sister, Melinda, reminded me of the Easter our beloved Papa Dude died and was buried on Easter Sunday. Mama had not had time to finish sewing the lace on her Easter dress and she had to go to the funeral lace-less. However, by the next Sunday Mama had completed said dress, lace and all. Papa Dude would have been proud!

I tried to carry on this sewing tradition with my own daughters making everything from cross-stitched sailor-collared creations to lacy, dotted-swiss masterpieces. I don't know how my Mama kept her sanity making three sometimes four dresses if she had the time or energy to make one for herself. By the time I was finished with two, I wanted to throw that Singer as far as I could fling it and swore never to attempt such a feat again in this lifetime. Until next Easter.

My Mama was a sewing saint. When I told her in August that my hubby-to-be and I had decided to get married in October, she quietly began to get things in order to make a wedding dress, two bridesmaid dresses, her mother-of-the-bride dress, and four bridal shower outfits. They just don't make Mamas like that anymore, at least not at my house.

Many of those fashion creations ended up in quilts made from the scraps of Easters gone by. Each quilt told a story and to this day I can tell you the significance of each square of my treasured quilts. I can tell you whose dress it came from and even the time and the occasion for said dress. I can almost smell the smells, taste the tastes, and hear the sounds of the occasion accompanying each quilt square. My husband categorizes his memories by music, but I by scraps of material long—faded but not forgotten.

Mama's Quilt

Mama's quilt is hanging in a place of honor
And it's on display for all our friends to see.
Each and every stitch and fabric
Is a memory of her life
And the love in Mama's heart for family.

In Mama's quilt there is a flowered piece of fabric.

Mama sewed that baby gown just for me.

A bit of sister's Easter dress

And a piece of Daddy's shirt

Stitched together like a family ought to be.

Mama's quilt it kept us warm on cold December nights

She would heat it by the fireplace 'cross the floor.

Then she'd wrap it all around us

As we snuggled in our beds.

Mama loved us, who could ask for any more?

Chorus:

Mama's quilt tells the story of our family;

Of my childhood playing at my Mama's knee;

Mama's gone to be with Jesus

She's at heaven's quilting bee,

But her quilt is a reminder

Of her love for family.

Chapter 18

Good Night, My Love
(Moonlight and Mosquitoes)

*W*hen I was a child, bedtime at our house followed a certain routine. Our Mama and Daddy gathered us together in the living room for devotions. That meant Scripture reading and reciting our own memory verses. My two sisters said the same two verses every night one right behind the other. I thought it was one verse until I was grown. "Jesus said, "I am the way, the truth, and the life" . . . "Be not afraid, only believe." My Daddy would pray and then it was off to bed.

On summer evenings there was another ritual. Because we had no air conditioning, the windows were up and the screens were such that mosquitoes shared the room with us. Consequently, we would soon be exposed to something that I am sure would now be considered child abuse . . . the dreaded mosquito poison! Daddy would come into the bedroom armed with the mosquito sprayer. It was a long cylinder attached to a can filled with DDT or some other equally lethal liquid. He pumped that noxious spray all over the room leaving a white fog of toxin lingering in the air. All the while we were hunkered down under the sheets which I am sure did absolutely nothing to protect our little lungs. I am convinced we inhaled more of the stuff than the EPA would deem safe and our bedroom would probably have been condemned as a toxic waste site. Nonetheless, we didn't have any mosquito bites!

The final ritual of the evening was our bedtime spanking. Sharing a bed with a sister usually meant that within an hour or so we would have laughed, giggled, and sometimes fought our way into the wrath of Daddy. We heard these words several times before he actually acted on them. "If you don't settle down in there, I'm coming with my belt!" He was always true to his word. And we were always prepared with lots of pillows under the sheets. After he was satisfied that he had sufficiently fulfilled the Scripture, "Spare the rod (or in our case, the belt) and spoil the child," we all settled down for a somewhat peaceful night of rest. After several minutes of searching for a cool place on the sheet, we were lulled to sleep by the drone of a dancing box fan until slumber overtook us. Ah, the comfort of home!

Chapter 19

Snow in the South

*W*e always had snow on Christmas morning at our house in the Deep South. You don't believe me? It's true! My Daddy made sure of it. Now it wasn't the white flakey stuff that on rare occasions fell from the sky in our neck of the woods. No, it was something much better than that . . . it was apple snow.

Christmas breakfast was a tradition of the Lumley clan and for as long as I can remember, a part of that tradition was apple snow. To my knowledge, my Daddy was the only one who could make it. The day before Christmas, he would carefully search the local Piggly Wiggly for two perfect Red Delicious apples. They had to be big, firm, shiny and beautiful. Christmas morning while the bacon, sausage, eggs, and grits were cooking, he would take six egg whites and whip them by hand until they stood like snow-covered mountains. To this, he would add a cup of sugar and a teaspoon of vanilla. Next, he would cut the apples in half lengthwise and remove the pulp and the seeds. He would then take a spoon, scrape out the sweet meat of the apples, and add it to the egg whites and sugar. Finally, he would beat that concoction by hand until it was so stiff that he could turn the bowl upside down and not lose a drop of snow. My sisters, Mary Sue and Melinda, and our cousin, Betty, always preferred to eat their snow with hot homemade biscuits, but I loved it right by itself.

Now that Daddy is gone I'm afraid his expertise for apple snow is gone also. However, I have promised myself that this year I am going to perfect the art of making apple snow, and as God is my witness, come Christmas we will once again have snow in the Deep South.

My sisters and I put our heads together to make sure we all remembered the same recipe for snow. In fact, they tried it out this past weekend and guess what . . . it snowed in Alabama in July! Here is the tried and true recipe for apple snow Lumley-style.

Apple Snow

2 shiny Red Delicious apples

6 egg whites

1 cup of sugar

1 tsp. vanilla

Beat egg whites stiff. Add the sugar and vanilla. Cut the apples lengthwise and remove pulp and seeds. Take a spoon and scoop out the meat of the apple. It should look like apple mush when you're done. Add the apple meat to the eggs and sugar and beat until you can turn the bowl upside down and your apple snow does not fall out. Serve with hot biscuits if you like. Like the real stuff, apple snow won't last. Eat immediately and don't try to store it in the fridge. It melts and turns to slush.

After researching apple snow on the internet, I discovered that it is an Irish dish, but our recipe is a little different from the two I found online. Ours is the Southern version!

Chapter 20

Cleaning Fish and Other Manual Labors

*M*y Mama gave me some good advice when I was about to become a married woman. Don't learn to clean fish, birds, or other varmints husbands bring home from a day at the hunt. At the time, I thought those were strange instructions coming from a woman whom I believed could do anything. However, I was soon to learn that it was some of the best advice I would ever get. A friend of mine puts it this way: "Start out like you can hold out!" Succinctly put, if you can't wait on him hand and foot till death do you part, you'd best not start out that way.

I began to think of how things can change after thirty years of marriage:

Year One: "*Oh, Sugah, you sit still and let me get you another glass of sweet tea.*"

Year Thirty: "*It's in the fridge where it always is. Something wrong with your legs?*

Year One: "*Don't bother to pick up your underwear. I'll get it and put it in the hamper, Sweetie!*"

Year Thirty: "*Let it lay there if you want, but come Friday you won't have any clean underwear, Stinky!*"

Year One: "*Oh, yes, Precious! I think that mustache looks dashing!*"

Year Thirty: "*You'd better shave off that pitiful fringe of hair you're calling a mustache if you think you're ever gonna kiss me again, Scruffy!*"

Year One: "*Why of course I'll take the car down to have the oil changed, Punkin. I love sitting at Lucky Lube all morning. It's so relaxing.*"

Year Thirty: "*The car's making a weird knocking sound and there's a black puddle in the driveway. Better take it to Lucky Lube (aptly named, as you will be lucky to get in and out of there in under four hours!). Smelling the grease down there makes me wanta throw up!*"

Year One: *"Oooh, what a beautiful string of fish! You just go sit in your Lazy Boy and I'll have those things cleaned and cooked before you know it. What a wonderful provider you are, My Big Ol'Hunk o'Man!*

Year Thirty: *(on the phone—because he knows better than to show up with a string of those malodorous things without some kind of warning) "What's that you say? You want fish for supper? Well, unless you plan to clean and cook those smelly things yourself, you'd better stop off at Freddie's Fried Fish and Fixins' for supper. And how about bringing me a carry out? I'll be in the Lazy Boy!*

Year One: *"Now Sweet Tater, I'm sure I can figure out how to cook a week's worth of delicious gourmet meals on $25. You just take that other $75 and go buy yourself a new fishing lure or something else equally important."*

Year Thirty: *"What's that you say? You want to know where all the grocery money is going? Just turn sideways and look in the mirror, Tater Tot!"*

Year One*: "Oh, Sweetie Pie, I just finished reading **How to Have a Happy Hubby** and I can't wait to show you what I've learned."*

Year Thirty*: "What book? **How to Have a Happy Hubby?** Oh, yeah, I think I lined the rabbit cage with it. You look pretty fat and happy to me, Romeo. Bless yore heart!"*

Chapter 21

Walmart, Kmart and Other Chic Boutiques

*S*hopping in the South is done almost exclusively at one of two mega-stores—Walmart, affectionately known as Wally World, and Kmart, sometimes referred to as Madame K's. Gives it a little class, don't you think? The motto of the South is "If they don't sell it at Wally World or Madame K's, then you don't need it." We like our one-stop shopping, from apples to air compressors, bread to boxers, corn to compost . . . you get the picture. It saves a lot of gas to be able to pick up whatever you need at one place, including gas. But, it wasn't always like this. When I was growing up, the bulk of the shopping was done on Saturday and the place was "downtown." From the far reaches of the county-lines, everybody loaded up and came to town on Saturday to shop and socialize. Friends visited as they stocked up on supplies from apples to air compressors, bread to boxers, corn to compost.

Downtown was kinda like a big ol' WalMart on those Saturdays. Some "chewed the fat" (translation—caught up on all the news around town) and some "chewed tobacco" and spit on the sidewalks (no translation needed). Others just leaned on storefronts and enjoyed the sights and sounds of a bustling little town alive with friends and relatives enjoying a reprieve from the never-ending hard work on the farm. My place on those wonderful Saturdays was in Tucker's Five and Dime Store mostly behind the candy counter selling bags of delicious chocolate-covered peanuts and other fresh confectionaries. I can still smell 'em . . . and taste 'em! This shopping frenzy would continue until well into the evening when tired but happy residents made their way back to their respective corners of the county to work hard for another week, always anticipating next Saturday's trip to town for apples and air compressors, bread and briefs, corn and compost . . .

Chapter 22

Shop 'Til You Drop

*S*outhern women love to shop, from WalMart to Riches, flea markets to high-end boutiques, Farmer's Markets to roadside stands. We know how to shop 'til we drop! In the spring and fall when the weather is "just right" we hit the outdoor venues hunting for bargains. When it's too hot or too cold, we search out the shopping comfort of the local mall. Shopping is a year-round sport for most of us and we do it in style. My Daddy always said that we would buy it if it was on sale whether we needed it or not. Duh, that's a given!

I believe shopping is a gift of the Spirit. I know it can certainly be a spiritual experience! However, after much searching of Paul's letters in Scripture, I do not find that gift listed with the other spiritual gifts. Hmmm . . . I think I figured it out. A man wrote that. It's not going to be included.

Have you ever had a dress just jump off the rack at you? And did you take that as a sign from above that the dress was sovereignly ordained to be yours? Then you probably have the Gift of Shopping. The day the dress jumped off the rack at me I bought it and took it home. Now, I don't know about your husband, but my preacher-husband doesn't look at anything before he looks at the price tag. Well, he took one look at that price tag and he had a Baptist fit right there in the bedroom. He said, "Fifty dollars? Why, we've never paid $50 for any piece of clothing!" I said, "I know, but I was tempted right there in the Mall!" He continued his rant by reminding me that the next time I was tempted I needed to quote this scripture: "Get thee behind me, Satan!" I explained to him that I had said those very words right there in the dressing room. I tried on that dress and I knew I was in trouble. I raised my hand to my invisible nemesis whom I am sure was right there in the dressing room with me and said in my firmest temptation-resisting voice, "Get thee behind me, Satan!" Then Satan said, "It looks good from back here, too. Buy it!"

I heard of one wife who enlisted her husband to go to the mall and purchase a bra for her. Lesson 1: Never send a man to do a woman's job! It usually does not end well. Amazingly, he agreed. When he arrived at the lingerie counter, he quietly asked the saleslady for a bra for his wife. She replied loudly, "What kind of bra would you like?" "There are different kinds?" he asked incredulously. "Why, of course! We have the Catholic bra, the Presbyterian bra, the Salvation Army bra, and the Baptist bra," she answered. "What is the difference?" he asked. "Well," she began, "The Catholic bra rounds up the masses, the Presbyterian bra keeps them staunch and upright, the Salvation Army bra lifts up the fallen, and the Baptist bra makes mountains out of mole hills." I know which one my husband would have bought!

Speaking of bras, I was always a bit unclear of the numbers and letters on the tag. Well, I guess I understand the numbers, it's the letters that trip me up. Just recently, a woman older and wiser than I explained them to me. Here is the list for your information:

A	*Almost*
B	*Barely*
C	*Cute*
D	*Dandy*
E	*Enormous*
F	*Fake*
G	*Gone South*
H	*Help me, I've fallen and I can't get up!*

So enamored with shopping am I that I wrote a song in honor of all those Southern ladies who have that spiritual gift and who regularly exercise it. Girls, this one's for you!

The Blue Light Special

(sung to the tune of "The Midnight Special")

Well I woke up Saturday morning

Had some shoppin' on my mind.

So I jumped into my Nissan

I was Dublin bound.

Got my checkbook in my pocket.

Don't you get in my way.

There ain't nothin' gonna stop me

Cause I'm headed to Big K.

Have you ever been shoppin'

And heard that voice from above?

"Well, ladies now the light's on

In hosiery and gloves."

Them ladies they'll fight you

Might even break your nose

Just to save a few dollars

On their panty hose.

There goes Mrs. Johnson

How'n the world did you know?

By the way she raced her buggy

And run down Mrs. Rowe.

Well, they called Mrs. Rowe's husband

To come and take her home.

But he was rushing down to hardware

'Cause the blue light was on.

Chorus:

Let the blue light special

Shine her light on me.

Let the blue light special

Shine her light on me.

Let the blue light special

Shine her light on me.

Let the blue light special

Shine her everlovin' light on me!

Chapter 23

Dumpster Diving

*N*ow you may find this odd, but I actually enjoy going to the dump. You see, I'm too economically conservative (translation: CHEAP) to pay someone to come to my house and pick up my trash when I am already going by the dump on my way to town. I'm not above a little inconvenience and grime to save a little money.

One morning as I was making my way to the dump to deliver a load of trash, I was busily talking on my cell phone. Imagine that! As I proceeded to chunk the bag of garbage into the dumpster, my cell phone sailed in with it. I was horrified! It was a brand new phone and you know that the reason I even go to the dump is my economical conservatism (CHEAPNESS)! I stood staring into the mouth of the big green monster that had just swallowed my cell phone. I knew what I had to do! I shouted to the gentleman in the car behind me, "Don't throw your trash in there yet . . . I've got to go in after *my cell phone!" He nodded in the affirmative, but I thought I heard him mutter under his breath, "Crazy woman!" I ran down to the little house where the dumpster man lives and asked for permission to go into the dumpster to retrieve my cell phone. He too nodded his consent, but again I thought I heard someone mutter, "Crazy woman!" Strangely, the dumpster man followed me back to the dumpster. By this time, the man who had been parked behind me had left his vehicle and joined us there. At first I thought I wasn't going to have to actually get in the dumpster. Surely, one of these fine Southern gentlemen would offer to rescue a Southern damsel in distress. Wrong! Both of them stood and stared as I hoisted myself up onto the ledge of the mouth of the big green monster and began to look around trying to spot the phone. I finally had to climb down inside the thing and walk around searching and feeling for my phone. Both men poked their heads in to help me "look" for it. Finally, the dumpster man yelled, "There it is!" Yes, I picked it up with my bare hands. I hadn't known I would need surgical gloves just to go to the dump that day. With phone in hand, I began to look for a way out of the dumpster. Guess what! There are no handles on the inside of a dumpster to help you climb out. After several attempts, I finally pulled myself out of the green monster and jumped to the ground. Those men were impressed I'm sure, but again I thought I heard someone mutter, "Crazy woman!"*

The next Sunday I was relaying my most recent saga of the Life and Times of Your Crazy Preacher's Wife to my Sunday School class of older adults. They seemed to enjoy hearing of my misadventures before we actually began the lesson. When I concluded the episode of "Dumpster Diving," Don, one of the precious men in the class said, "Well, that explains everything. Just last week a friend of mine was driving by the dump on Oak Hill Road and he said someone had thrown out a perfectly good woman!" This time I know I heard someone mutter, "Crazy woman!"

When we moved to Dublin, I was dreading having to break in a new dumpsite and a new set of dumpster attendants. To my delight, it wasn't hard at all. Two of the sweetest men work at my new dump. Joe and Gene are some of the most encouraging fellows you'd ever want to meet. Every time I go to the dump I ask Joe, "How are you doing today?" His answer is always, "I'm holding on!" Just this past Saturday we exchanged the same pleasantries as always, but this time I said, "Joe, what are you holding on to? (I know that's a dangling something or other, but that's the way we talk in the South!) He raised his hand toward heaven and said, "I'm holding on to God's unchanging hand!" Who knew you could be spiritually uplifted just going to the dump! When Gene is on duty, he always pretends to fuss about how we Southern women jump out of the car and start dumping our own garbage before he can get there to help. But then he always says, "I like strong Southern women!" Me, too! I'll bet I wouldn't have had to get in the big green monster if Gene or Joe had been around.

Chapter 24

Party Naked

*E*ven good clean Southern living will not protect you from some downright embarrassing situations. In fact, I seem to be a magnet for awkward circumstances, i.e., the dumpster episode. The good thing is that these experiences have taught me a valuable lesson. I have learned to laugh at myself. Southerners as a whole are a happy, upbeat crowd of folks. Maybe it's because we have learned to laugh at ourselves in all kinds of situations.

I remember one such instance in my life. As a teacher, I was called upon to attend an assortment of meetings. One afternoon as I was preparing to travel to a countywide meeting at a neighboring school, I realized I had left my sunglasses at home. I swung by a service station to get gas and to pick up a pair of shades. Because I was in a hurry, I just grabbed a black pair off the rack, paid for them, and was on my way.

When I got to the neighboring school, I perched those glasses on top of my head and sat through a long and uninteresting meeting. Following that meeting I decided to head on over to another school to attend a Quiz Bowl Meet in which my middle school daughter was competing. Before I left the first meeting, I asked one of the guys in the parking lot for directions to the next school. Along with the directions, he gave me a quizzical look that I would understand later. I slipped in to the Quiz Bowl Meet a little late, again with the sunglasses on top of my head. At the end of the meet, I was congratulating my daughter and her team when one of her friends said, "Miss Elaine, why do you have those glasses on?" I thought she meant that they were ugly. I explained that I had just grabbed them off the rack and I knew that they weren't the coolest glasses on the rack. She said, "No, that's not what I mean. Why do you have sunglasses with PARTY NAKED! written on the side?" Horrified, I jerked them off my head and to my dismay sure enough PARTY NAKED was written in bright white lettering down one side. I was mortified for a second and then I exploded in uncontrollable laughter. Now remember, I am a Baptist preacher's wife. Not exactly what you'd expect from one who should hold such a dignified position in the community. I laughed all the way home! I recalled what my principal had said to me just before I left for the meeting, "Now don't embarrass me at that meeting!" Now where did that come from? You'd think I made a habit of embarrassing myself in public! Go figure! The next morning when I got to school, I went straight to his office with those sunglasses on my head and said, "Do you think this would embarrass you?" He just rolled his eyes and said, "You didn't tell anybody which school you're from, did you?" This was too good not to share and share I did! One of my friends went on vacation that summer and brought me back a red visor with the words PARTY NAKED written in bold black letters on the front. I wear it proudly with my PN sunglasses. FYI: In the South there is a distinction between naked and nekkid. If you're naked, you're clothesless, but if you're nekkid, you're clothesless and doing something of which your Mama would not approve. Good thing my glasses said NAKED!

I would love to be able to tell you that with age comes wisdom and the end of such foolishness as that. But, just tonight as I was hanging up my clothes from church, I caught a glimpse of the tag in my skirt and realized I had worn it backward all day long. I wondered why it had those two flaps in the front! Oh, well, I probably wouldn't have a comedy ministry or material for this book if I wasn't blessed with howlers like these! Laugh long and prosper!!!!

Chapter 25

To Everything There Is A Season

I believe we are blessed in the South to have four distinctly recognizable seasons: spring, summer, fall, and winter. I don't think I would like living where it is always cold or always hot. I like my warm springs, hot summers, cool falls, and cold winters. For the most part Southern weather cooperates and stays in its proper season. However, we have been known to have 90 degree temps in November and 50 degree temps in June. That's another good thing about Southern seasonal weather. It'll surprise you! What girl doesn't like surprises? If you don't like the weather in the South, just stick around a little while and it'll change right before your very eyes.

I have discovered something very unique about the South. We have other seasons equally important, if not more so. There's football season, basketball season, baseball season, deer season (bow and gun), Nascar *season, bird season, duck season, and turkey season just to name a few. In fact, those who find great sport in the hunt find these seasons more appealing than the four weather-related ones.*

Whether it's the local high school team or the college team of choice, the first football game of the season is often met with as much anticipation as Christmas morning, with local home-town games eliciting as much excitement as the Super Bowl. I've known some folks who couldn't sleep for nights before the kickoff of their favorite team's season, i.e., Clark, Anthony and Alton. My college team of choice is the University of Georgia Bulldogs. The proper response at the mention of the letters UGA would be to remove your hat and place it over your left shirt pocket of Skoal for a moment. There is another team in our state which some consider to be worthy of their allegiance, though the logic for that escapes me. However, I will mention Georgia Tech out of respect for some of my closest family and friends, misguided as they may be. Every Southern town and region takes great pride in wearing their team's colors and yelling themselves hoarse in support of their boys. I've even known some fans to carry their unbridled allegiance to the parking lot afterwards with something more tangible than words. Southerners are proud folks and will gladly let you know it when it comes to football. Whether it's Friday night high school football or Saturday afternoon college games, both are times of anticipation, enthusiasm, celebration, and camaraderie almost reaching the emotional level of a Pentecostal camp meeting. Some folks will tell you that the three denominations in the South are Baptist, Methodist, and UGA football. You know there are only a few letters difference in the words fan and fanatic. Southern fans can become fanatics in just about the time it takes to add the extra letters. Go, Dawgs!

Baseball season is as religiously observed and enjoyed as football season with the Atlanta Braves team becoming the summertime mania in Georgia. There's nothing better than a hot summer day at the ballpark. Lots of hotdogs, Coca-Cola (that includes every brand of soda; we call them all Coca-Cola), peanuts, nachos and other stadium treats fill our stomachs for nine or more innings of fun interrupted only by the seventh inning stretch of "Take Me Out to the Ballgame." It don't get no better than that! Lousy English, but great Southernese! See you at the game!

I'm not much for basketball but that is the sport that floats a lot of boats in the South. These die-hard fans live for the Final Four and spend every waking hour trying to figure out who'll make it and who'll foul out. Again, the fervor of these fans rivals that of a Tent Revival. Hallelujah!

I would certainly be remiss if I didn't mention Nascar Racing Season, a sport that at one time was dominated by good old redneck Southern drivers who'd just as soon whoop 'em off the track as on. It was not uncommon to see drivers of days gone by bang and crash their way around the track climaxing in an all-out brawl at the finish line. Those were the days! These days it is not uncommon to hear non-southern accents coming out of those helmets and sponsors like 'Save the Whales' tattooed on the hoods of those speedy machines. Sad, isn't it?

Update: I have just returned from a night at the races . . . NASCAR wannabe style. I was wrong. Good old-fashioned get down and dirty racin', dirt-track style, still exists. I sat in the stands among lots of folks sporting too much exposed skin with all sorts of body graffiti out there for God and everybody to see. They were dipping into swayback coolers full of all kinds of refreshments. And we were all breathing in more than what I am sure is a healthy amount of dirt-saturated air. To tell you the truth, I felt as if I had stepped back forty years in time. Maybe all is not lost in racing today! Gentlemen (and I use that term loosely), start your engines!

Deer Season (bow and gun) is a distinct season as surely as spring, summer, fall, and winter. You are likely to find as many bow and gun fanatics tossing and turning the night before opening day as you would wide-eyed children on Christmas Eve. This concerns me a bit that come break of opening morn the woods are full of sleep-deprived men armed with live ammunition in search of anything that moves. I found this to be true when we lived in Mississippi. Many a Sunday morning the forest around our church in the midst of the piney woods rang out not with church bells but with the sound of deer rifles trailing an unsuspecting would-be mount. In fact, during deer season I found out the hard way that the dump was a dangerous place to be at the height of the season. More than once I have been dumping my garbage only to be surrounded by the sounds of hunters on the move. I'm afraid they would have been sorely disappointed with their trophy had they bagged me. I don't think I would look good mounted on a wall. Gee, I didn't realize that my affinity for dumps went back that far.

And last, but not least, there are bird, duck, and turkey seasons all effecting the same heightened sense of primal urgency to kill it and/or cook it or mount it. It is ironic that a southern gentleman who is not easily awakened on an average Saturday morning will bound out of bed long before dawn without the assistance of a single Bonk! from an alarm clock. This same man who fusses about taking out the garbage will sit out in the cold and damp fields making strange noises on man-made callers to attract the attention of some gullible fowl that will hopefully become dinner or decoration. Guess you had to be there!

Chapter 26

Squirrel Killin' Time

Varmints were not just hunted and killed in the wide-open woods and fields. Sometimes we had to get 'em right in the confines of the holy place. We had a serious problem with squirrels that had invaded our solemn assembly and turned it into their playground. For several months we had tried everything we knew to rid the church of this horde of nut-nibbling mischief-makers who was turning Sunday morning worship into a carnival. As we tried to worship they ran in herds through the attic of the building sounding more like rogue elephants than bushy-tailed rodents. They chewed through the wiring of our sound system, ate through a gas line almost blowing us all to kingdom come, and made a mess of our insulation. There was talk of a lynching if only they could catch one. Someone suggested trapping one and starving him to death in the church parking lot. It was said that the sound he would make as he died a slow and painful demise would alert all other squirrels to stay away from this death camp. Sounds horrible, doesn't it? We didn't try that because we knew the Humane Society would frown on such savagery. That was not the kind of publicity we wanted.

On the Sunday before Christmas, the squirrel crisis came to a head. The choir had gathered in the Fellowship Hall to warm up before our biggest performance of the year, our Christmas Cantata. As I was giving the last pep talk before our presentation, two of our deacons motioned for me to come to the door. Joe and Mack had bad news. One of our four-footed troublemakers had escaped the confines of the attic and was loose in the worship center. All I could think of was Ray Steven's song about the Mississippi Squirrel. I looked them dead in the eye and said, "Get rid of him!" Obediently, they disappeared down the hall. What happened next? I can only tell you what I was told. From all accounts, this is how it went down. Joe went home and retrieved a gun loaded with rat shot. Meanwhile, Mack cornered the poor defenseless squirrel in the broom closet in the back of the church. Quietly, so as not to alarm anyone, the two deacons asked the preacher and his Sunday School class who were meeting on the back pews of the church, to move down to the front. They complied and I am told that what happened next would have terrified the bravest of Christian soldiers. Joe aimed, fired, and with one sure blast of rat-shot, the Good Lord called that little squirrel home. I'm glad I did not know until later that our Cantata was presented within the very confines of a bonafide yellow-tape crime scene. When the preacher asked them why on earth they would shoot a squirrel in a church closet, both men answered, "Your wife told us to!" I have been blamed for a lot of things as a pastor's wife, but that was the first time I had been accused of accessory to murder. Where else but in the South would you find squirrel huntin' deacons shootin' 'em right in the middle of the church house on the Lord's Day all at the behest of the preacher's wife herself!?! I can't make this stuff up. Truth is truly stranger (and more fun) than fiction!

I suppose the moral of this story is:

Be glad you're not a squirrel when the deacons are carrying guns!

Chapter 27

Sun-Worshippers

*E*verybody in the South knows that tanned fat is much more attractive than winter-white fat. It also appears to be much thinner . . . thus our affinity for sunbathing, aka bronzing the buttocks, tanning the tail, laying out, etc. At the first hint of warm weather, the Southern sun-worshippers would douse themselves with anything from Crisco (not a good idea!) to the name-brand products which promised a deep, dark tan in hours. It was a daily afternoon ritual on my college campus to snag one of the highly prized rooftop spots to sizzle and flip your epidermis to a golden brown. The race was on! Who could be the loveliest shade of deep, dark brown before summer even arrived?

Not only was it a college ritual it was one that was played out in our own backyard. Day after day we "laid out" amidst ants, bugs, and itchy grass to perfect that ideal shade of tanned skin. My aunt's friend *would always shout out the back door when she came to visit, "That sun's gonna give you skin cancer!" We were annoyed and wished she would keep her opinions to herself. We were certain her words were just Old Wives' Tales and would amount to nothing. We broiled at the beach, baked in the backyard, crisped at the corner pool, and sizzled at the seaside. We even kidded ourselves into thinking that tanning beds were harmless and we could still get that healthy tanned body without the dangerous side effects of the sun. I'm afraid we've been proven wrong and now we are paying for it with wrinkles, spots, and regular visits to the dermatologist hoping that our worship ritual of college days does not reap a diagnosis of skin cancer.*

We've come a long way from the days of gentle Southern belles who went to great lengths to cover their delicate white skin so as not to develop the tan of a field hand. I'm beginning to get the idea that they were smarter than today's knowledgeable and educated woman. Chalk one up for our fore-sistahs!

Chapter 28

Sisters . . . Or If You're From the South
SISTAHS

*H*ave you ever had something *happen to you that was so hilariously funny you almost wet your panties and maybe you did? Then did you try to recount it to your precious husband and expect him to laugh uproariously with you? And did you get a blank stare from that darling man as if to say, "Duh, I don't get it!" Then did he mutter this response, "Guess you had to be there." Girl, tell a sistah 'cause men don't get it! Whatever "it" is, they just don't get it! They can't really help it, so don't be too hard on them. They just don't have what it takes to realize and recognize the truly important things in life like we women do.*

Notice I used the word 'sistah' rather than 'girlfriend.' That's because there is a difference. Girlfriends are the assortment of friends and acquaintances with whom you share a certain level of friendship, but sistahs are the kind that are closer than marrow. In my circle of sistahs we not only share a bond of familiarity, we share a bond of family. That bond is the kinship we share through the Blood of Christ. We truly are blood kin. Let me explain, I have two flesh and blood sisters, two flesh and blood daughters, and a whole passel of flesh and blood female relatives. That is the flesh and blood kin bond. Those same flesh and blood relatives are also my sistahs in Christ because of the blood kinship we share through Him. Get it? Then there are all those sistahs who are not blood kin in the familial way, but are just as close because of the blood of Christ kinship. Are you there yet? I guess you truly do have to have be there to get it! If you have figured out what I have been trying to explain in a somewhat rambling fashion, then you have discovered one of the greatest treasures about being a Southern woman. We do love our sistahs! They are precious to us in the best sense of that word. What would we do without our sistahs?

From the time we were able to tell the difference between boys and girls, we realized that the female variety of our species operates on a different level than the male. You generally don't have to teach little boys to like little boy things, nor do you have to teach little girls to like little girl things. Most of us just know! Why is that? Because male and female brains don't work the same. In other words, we are wired differently. That's why sistahs understand sistahs better than anybody else on the planet. From the male perspective, we can have some of the strangest conversations. Listen to this:

> *Sistah 1: Hey, Sistah! I just got back from . . .*
>
> *Sistah 2: Hon, I know. That was the best . . .*
>
> *Sistah 1: You bet is was and those . . .*
>
> *Sistah 2: Weren't they wonderful? And so . . .*
>
> *Sistah 1: Yeah, how do they . . .*
>
> *Sistah 2: Beats me, but they sure did . . .*
>
> *Sistah 1: I know, and can you believe . . .*
>
> *Sistah 2: I wouldn't have if I hadn't seen . . .*
>
> *Sistah 1: Bless her heart!*
>
> *Sistah 2: Yeah, she's so . . .*
>
> *Sistah 1 and 2: Precious!*

Only a sistah could understand that conversation. After listening to that feminine dialogue a man would only shake his head and mutter under his breath, "Guess you had to be there."

U\PDATE:

Just last week I was talking to my Bible Study group about this very thing and I heard a story that just might offer a glimmer of hope for

*clueless mates. As we were discussing how men don't generally "get it,"
I noticed Christy nodding and laughing. Then she shared this experience
with us. She had come home from a day of great bargain shopping and
was thrilled to have bought twenty items for only twenty dollars. She
was enthusiastically sharing this news with her young hunter-husband.
The initial look of "guess you had to be there" gave way to a grin and
this revelation, "You just got a big buck, didn't you!" Hallellujah, there
is hope!!*

*Several years ago our Women's Ministry Team decided we needed
some time away for planning, praying, and shopping, of course. It just so
happened that I had a show in Knoxville, Tennessee and a dear friend of
ours had a beautiful home on the top of a nearby mountain. We decided
to mix business (mine) with pleasure (theirs) and spend our getaway
there. We did what all sistahs do when we get away. We ate too much,
slept too little, laughed until we cried, cried until we laughed again,
and got a little planning done on the side. It had been a fantastic girls'
weekend away!*

*On the last morning we were there, I awoke earlier than the others
and quietly slipped out to sit on the deck. The early morning scenery
was breathtaking! We were so high on the mountain that a misty layer
of fog and clouds had completely covered the valley below. It really felt
like we were insulated from the world beneath us. I couldn't stand not
sharing this with the others, so I went inside and woke them to come*

and marvel at what God had done for us that morning. After awhile we decided that the view would be even better with some food and the two Martha's began to prepare breakfast. The rest of us were keeping them company while they worked. All of a sudden, I had the strangest feeling come over me. A strange numbness went down my whole right side. I shook it off as well as I could and didn't say anything to anybody. After a while I knew I had to tell somebody because I wasn't sure but what I was going to die right there on top of those clouds. I finally asked if anybody had an aspirin. I figured it was either a heart attack or a stroke and had heard that aspirin was good for one of them. When my sistahs realized that I was really in trouble, they sprang into action. Now if you have never seen a group of deeply spiritual women rev up their unique gifts to help a sistah in her time of trouble, then you have missed an awesome sight. Fran and Pat were praying, Linnelle had a cold cloth on my forehead and was unbuckling my belt (I'm not sure which gift that was!), and Sue was calling 911. I looked around at my wonderful sistahs and thought that it might not be so bad to die here among people who cared and seemed to love me. Then I realized that Marilyn, my single friend, was nowhere to be seen. Now Marilyn and I have been close for a long time. We live in the same neighborhood and have been walking together for years. If I hadn't been so afraid that I was having "the big one" I probably would have been hurt that Marilyn was not by my side in my last moments. I was feeling a little better when we heard the faint whine of a siren in the distance. I finally asked, "Where's Marilyn?" This is what I was told. When Marilyn heard that paramedics would be coming, she headed downstairs to put on her make-up. Who knew, they might be single! I have forgiven Marilyn for putting her chance to snag a man above our friendship. And I'm sure that one day God will, too!

Chapter 29

A Sistah for Eve

I *heard about an elderly lady who was asked, "Who is the first person you want to see when you get to heaven?" She replied without a moment's hesitation, "Eve." "And why would you want to see Eve first?" she was asked. "So I can beat the dickens out of her!" was her reply. Poor Eve, she gets blamed for all our woes just because she took a bite of that forbidden fruit. I have a theory about that if you'd care to hear it. The Bible says that God told Adam not to eat of that tree. It never says He told Eve. I suppose Adam was like every husband since then. He forgot to tell his wife something really, really important. And if he did relay the message, he must have left out some important details. Can anybody identify with that? Therefore, Eve's off the hook in my book.*

Seriously, I do feel sorry for Eve. After all, the only person she had to talk to was Adam, a man. I believe this dietary temptation incident might have turned out differently if only Eve had been blessed with a sistah with whom to discuss her fruity dilemma. It might have gone something like this:

Eve: *I'm bored . . . there's nothing to do in this garden.*

Sistah: *Girl, are you kidding me? This place is perfect.*

> *You've got the only man in town . . . and he's just about the most perfect man alive! You don't have to worry about clothes or food or security or anything.*

Eve: *I know all that . . . but I want something more!*

Sistah: *What more could you want?*

Eve: *I don't know . . . I just know something's missing. (Huge sigh) I'm just not HAPPY!*

Sistah: *How could you not be happy? You've got it all!*

Eve: *I know. I've got everything but—that tree. I wonder how the fruit from that tree tastes?*

(Let's just assume at this point that Adam did mention something about that tree.)

Sistah: Look here, Sistah. You know what Adam said about that tree. It's

off limits. It's no good for you. You'd better get that look out of your

eye and stay away from that tree!

Eve: I know all that. I just wonder . . .

(Enter the Serpent)

Sir Pent: Hey, girls . . . I just heard you talking about that tree. I don't

blame you, Eve, for wanting to know what that fruit is like. Let's go

find out!

Sistah (Grabbing Eve by the arm): It's that smooth-talking Sir Pent

again, Eve. Let's get out of here! He's nothing but trouble! Eve, are

you listening to me, Girl? (Well, this isn't working . . . he has her

undivided attention! There's just one thing that'll break his tempting

spell!) Eve, I hear there's a 75% off sale over at Garden Ridge and

they're giving away free chocolate . . . Let's go!

All of a sudden, the mention of a sale and free chocolate breaks the

spell of the serpent and all of humanity is saved from the FALL!!!!! I

rest my case!

Chapter 30

Steel Magnolias

I was first introduced to the expression "Steel Magnolias" when I saw the movie by the same title. I laughed 'til I cried and cried 'til I laughed as six strong Southern women faced life's challenges with a strength only Southern women know. I tried to adapt that concept to a uniquely Georgian idiom but somehow Georgia Granites and Petrified Peaches just didn't have the same appeal. So with Robert Harling's permission I will borrow that phrase and apply it to the Southern women I know. From lifelong observation and female insight, I believe strong yet gentle Steel Magnolias share these qualities:

S is for Strength. Southern women know that purely human strength is not enough to be overcomers. We know that we must draw our strength from God and from His Word. This is my verse of choice for the strength *needed to make it through the day. "I can do all things through Christ who strengthens me." Philippians 4:13*

T is for Trust, the kind that gives you Someone to lean on who will never let you down. I've learned that my wisdom is just not enough. I can get in all kinds of trouble if I am leaning on my own pitiful understanding. I'd rather trust the One who sees the whole picture and knows how it all ends. Makes me feel much more confident when I follow His advice and just "Trust in the Lord with all my heart and lean not on my own understanding . . ." Proverbs 5:5 Trust, Sistah!

E is for Encouragement. Where would we be without our sistahs to encourage us? Everybody needs an "Atta Girl" every now and then. Southern girls know what a kick-start it is to have someone sincerely compliment them on their whatever. We know how to build our sistahs up by giving them the courage to keep on keepin' on. How about this verse to remind us to be encouragers? "Therefore encourage one another and build one another up, just as you are doing." I Thessalonians 5:11

E is for End. Southern women know that everything must end. We know that for everything sweet and lovely, there is a final time. We don't dwell on it, we just realize it and prioritize life with that reality in mind.

L is for Love with all your heart. One thing about Southern women . . . we love with our whole being. We are passionate about *almost everything. We truly take to heart what Jesus Himself said, "Love the Lord your God with **all your heart, soul, and mind**. And love your neighbor as much as you love yourself." Don't be afraid to love like there's no tomorrow!*

M is for Move on! Steel Magnolias knows that no matter what happens to us in life, we must move on. Yes, we might fall apart, pitch a hissy fit or two, rant and rave over the unfairness of life, and make everybody around us miserable for a little while. Eventually we gather all the broken pieces and with the help of our sistahs, we glue them back together with love and prayer. Does that mean that we never look back or have a melancholy feeling? No. Do we ever lose a piece every now and then and have to be glued back together? Absolutely! And then we move on and continue following the God of Another Day.

A is for Acknowledge. Proverbs 5:6 exhorts us "In all your ways acknowledge Him and He will direct your paths." What does it mean to acknowledge Him? It means to see Him for Who He really is, see yourself for who you really are, and realize that your only position before Him is lying face down at His feet in worship. If you can get that picture in your head, then you will be ready to allow Him to direct your paths.

G is for Grit and Grin. A very wise woman whom we knew and loved in Mississippi answered the preacher's question, "How do you stay married for 60 years?" this way. Aunt Winnie said, "Well, Preacher, sometimes you've just gotta grit your teeth, grin and bear it!" I know he was expecting a sweet answer from a sweet saint, but I like the answer he got much better. Southern women know how to grit their teeth, grin, and bear whatever their load is. Being able to show those pearly whites even in the midst of trials and tribulations is the trademark of a true Steel Magnolia.

N is for Never say never! Change is a part of life and if you're not willing to change you'll either be left standing in the middle of the tracks or you'll be flattened by the train. Some things need to change, some things are changing now, but some things never change. Pray for wisdom to know which is which and act accordingly.

O is for Order. I serve a God of order and I believe He expects order in my life as much as my feminine brain will allow it. Does this mean rigidity? Absolutely not! It just means that by following His Word we make the effort to bring a little organization into our chaos. Remember there is an end to all of this and the more ordered our steps are the more we can accomplish for Him.

L is for Laugh a Lot!! It's good for you body, soul, and spirit. Every Southern woman knows that the cheapest face-lift we'll ever get is when we smile, smile, smile. And we also know that frowning causes wrinkles. 'Nuff said!

I is for Initiate. You won't find a Southern woman standing around waiting for life to happen. We're the ones orchestrating the next chapter. We might appear to be the weaker sex, but don't get in our way when we are on a mission. We like our men strong, but don't expect us to sit idly by and miss all the fun of living life to its fullest! Initiate, Initiate, Initiate!

Finally, A is for Accept. At the end of the day, no matter what life has thrown at us, we will accept the inevitable. We will bow in submission to God's will for our lives and we will bravely accept what He knows to be our destiny. We will accept others, warts and all, knowing that they, too, have a destiny to fulfill.

Take these insights from a Southern woman who loves and appreciates other Southern women.

Chapter 31

My Steel Magnolia Hall of Famers

*L*illian Ruth Smith Lumley, my mother in love and birth was the epitome of a gracious, strong, Southern woman. After losing my precious Daddy, she carried on in the tradition of the strongest of Smith women before her. She may have lost the Alzheimer battle but she won the final war with death, and even now enjoys the spoils of that hard fought victory in the heavenly places with her Jesus.

Kathryn Estine Blizzard Brantley, my mother in love and marriage, is another gracious, strong Southern woman who continues to carry on after losing her precious husband. Her way was marked before her by her sweet little Mama, Bertie Hutcheson Blizzard. Though she struggles with ailments that come from eighty-four years of life, she presses on to the high calling of her sweet Jesus.

Mary Sue Lumley Couch, my oldest sister, triumphed over tragedy after losing her young husband of only a few weeks in a terrible train accident in which she was also severely injured. God graciously restored her by giving her a wonderful mate and three fantastic children. Just recently, she walked through that valley of the shadow again when she lost her precious firstborn son, Christopher. I have observed that moving on after his death has been one painful step at a time, but it has all been forward. You are my hero, Big Sis!

Melinda Ruth Lumley Coghlan, my middle sister, stepped up when my Mama went home to be with Jesus and became the glue that holds this family together even now. She keeps us close, holds our hands and our hearts, listens with an untiring ear, and has more than once kept me from driving off a cliff. You are my rock, Sis!

Susan Kathryn Brantley Dailey, my treasured firstborn, longed for a child for several years. I watched as she cheered her friends on and supported them throughout their pregnancies, even though the desire of heart was not fulfilled. God blessed that gracious attitude with her very own gift from Him just a year ago from the writing of this book. Precious Levi has brought us all joy! Thank you, Lord! Your deep love and loyalty are precious jewels! Love on, Sweet Daughter!

Kati Rebecca Brantley Ayotte, my treasured secondborn, has the tenacity of a pitbull and the heart of a crusader. She is the one who speaks her mind in love, helps me to see the other side of every situation, keeps me accountable to what I say I believe, and makes me laugh, laugh, laugh. March on, Proud Daughter!

Rosemary Mayfield Gibbs, my cousin and friend, has been my traveling buddy and confidante, my friend and my partner in crime. She is another in a long line of strong Smith women who after losing a life-long mate bravely faced the challenge and triumphed. You go, Girl!

My two favorite women of the Bible, Ruth and Esther, exhibited strong steel magnolia characteristics back before the term was coined. Ruth was a Gentile woman who married a Jewish man and became one of only a few women named in the genealogy of Jesus. Esther was a Jewish woman who married a Gentile king and became a heroine who delivered her people from certain death. They may not have said 'y'all' or 'bless your heart', but they were nonetheless strong women in the tradition of the South (the Southern Kingdom of Judah, that is!).

I have discovered over the past few months that I am not a steel magnolia, perhaps aluminum or tin, but not steel. However, I have been and am blessed to be associated with some of the steeliest (I know that's not a word, but it works here) of magnolias. I started strong, though I am not convinced at this point that I will finish strong. Nevertheless, this I know, because of the strength and support I draw from other SM's, finish I will! I may limp over the finish line scarred, bruised and battered, but in the words of that famous Southerner, Miss O'Hara, as God is my witness, I will finish!

"I have fought a good fight, I have finished my course, I have kept the faith." II Timothy 4:7

See you at the Finish Line!

Your Southern Sistah

Rose Elaine Lumley Brantley

CPSIA information can be obtained at www.ICGtesting.com
Printed in the USA
LVOW06s0430031213

363578LV00001B/5/P